To my wonderful parents, who built my nest with
love, guidance, kindness, and generosity.

Free Range
MAMA

Kizzi

authorHOUSE®

AuthorHouse™ UK
1663 Liberty Drive
Bloomington, IN 47403 USA
www.authorhouse.co.uk
Phone: 0800.197.4150

Published by AuthorHouse 10/08/2018

ISBN: 978-1-5462-9465-8 (sc)
ISBN: 978-1-5462-9466-5 (hc)
ISBN: 978-1-5462-9464-1 (e)

Library of Congress Control Number: 2018908186

Print information available on the last page.

Epigraph

I asked God to take away my pain.
God said, no.
It is not for me to take away, but for you to give up.
I asked God to make my handicapped child whole.
God said, no.
Her spirit is whole, her body is only temporary.
I asked God to grant me patience.
God said, no.
Patience is a byproduct of tribulations; it isn't granted, it is learned.
I asked God to give me happiness.
God said, no.
I give you blessings. Happiness is up to you.
I asked God to spare me pain.
God said, no.
Suffering draws you apart from worldly cares and brings you closer to me.
I asked God to make my spirit grow.
God said, no.
You must grow on your own, but I will prune you to make you fruitful.
I asked God to help me LOVE others, as much as he loves me.
God said ... Ahhhh, finally, you get the idea.

> —Anonymous author taken from *Lifting the Veil of Duality* by
> Andreas Moritz

Foreword by Mary Daniels

When Kizzi first asked if I would be up for writing her foreword, I immediately felt honoured, humbled, and—I won't lie—a little surprised. I thought, "What do I know about an empty nest?" My twenty-one-year-old son was still at home, and, as much as I love him, his long trail of existence in the form of socks, trainers, and crockery was at times annoyingly noticeable. In fact, having been a full-time mum to one and part-time mum to three others since the young age of twenty-one, the thought of having an empty nest often conjured up joyful visions of running around my seaside flat naked with my favourite songs piping away in the background. However, as I write this, I really get it and feel it. A few months ago, my son moved out. Born and bred in London, he was no longer content with this sleepy seaside town and got itchy feet. My idea of heaven was slowly becoming his idea of hell.

Initially, I was OK. I kept busy with work trips and business. After a few weeks working from home, I began to feel the emptiness, especially when I passed his closed bedroom door. For the last several years, it had just been the two of us. Whilst he has always been pretty independent, we are very close and have been through a lot together. I miss his voice, his sarcasm, his sharing little bits of his day and asking for advice about work. He isn't always the chattiest soul in the world, but we laughed a lot, albeit mostly at each other. He was great company, and I just love him to bits.

In short, I really see the need for this book. I am so excited that Kizzi has found the strength and courage to open up about her own incredible journey. The way she touches on the various forms of what an *empty nest* can look like, and the amount of love, wisdom, and care she has put into this process, really shows. Her desire to guide her readers through every step of their journey is admirable and consistently stood out for me throughout the pages. Baring yourself—the good, the bad, and the ugly—in print is not as easy as people think, especially as you know that once it is out there it is really out there. Kizzi's step-by-step guide and insight into how she has rebuilt her life will be invaluable to so many women (and men) still wondering where to start.

I know, trying to move on and rediscover who you really are (once the need to be a 24/7 parent is gone) can be really challenging, but my hope is that Kizzi's rollercoaster of a journey gives you a few pointers in the right direction. Kizzi, I take my hat off to you. What an incredible journey you have been on! And, to all you 'mamas' just getting used to an empty nest, enjoy this, keep going, and, as Kizzi says so beautifully throughout her book, 'remember that you are never alone'!

With love,
Mary Daniels
Speaker, Storyteller, Coach and Crazy Wild Woman.
(Hay House Author of *Wild Awakening: 9 Questions that saved my life*)

Preface

Many people have asked me for advice over the years, just as I have asked many for theirs. Eventually I noticed a pattern emerging in the various people who were seeking healing or counsel from me. Something was missing in their lives. They may have had more money than they could ever spend in a hundred lifetimes, or be part of the happiest family one could dream of. They may have been homeless, walking the country from one church to another as does a Franciscan monk. But there was still something missing.

Have you heard the story of a hermit who lived in a cave close to a village and was one day confronted by an angry crowd of villagers? They accused him of having made a young girl pregnant. 'Is that so?' he asked. He took the young girl in and looked after her and the child. Some time passed, and the young girl went back to the village and confessed to her parents that she had lied; the son of their neighbour was, in fact, the father. The villagers went back to the hermit and apologised profusely, telling him they now knew the truth. 'Is that so?' he said.

I love this story because the monk deals with emotions on so many levels, yet he remains cool. He teaches us humility, which is inspirational. His life has been turned upside down, twice, yet he carries on without bitterness, anger, or hate. What a way to live a life.

I want this book to inspire people to go out and do something worthwhile with their life, to find meaning, especially in serving others. We all need a reason to get out of bed.

So crack open your shell, and leave your nest to become a *free range mama* by wandering along a path that makes you feel good and takes you to a destination you may only have dreamed of. Or you never knew existed.

Contents

Introduction

CRY, CRY, CRY; REPEAT

'He's gone,' my husband said. I'd just given birth to my first and only daughter, my third child. Twenty-three hours later, while I was still attached to the various tubes that a caesarean demand, my dad died. They never got to meet.

Hormones can be difficult—especially if you don't pay them, my husband jests. But when you give birth, you have a lot of happy hormones racing through your veins (progesterone, oxytocin, prolactin). When you lose someone, you have different hormones racing through your blood, and then you have a pile-up when they meet each other.

The loss of a parent is a huge weight to bear even though the passage of time makes it easier. We all know that one day we will depart this earth, but we don't know where or when or how we will feel when our mum or dad goes—until the actual event.

We also know that one day our fledglings, our little children, will grow up and leave us. Fleeing the nest is part of life's rich tapestry. And we also don't know how we will feel until that time comes.

For some of us, *empty nest syndrome* is a huge loss, a sense of bereavement. I had no idea what to expect when my little boy walked out the front door at age nineteen, wearing his backpack and a huge smile, which I reciprocated though my heart was breaking.

'He's gone,' my husband said. Again.

And the pain was quite extraordinary.

Although I know I'll be seeing my son again, I felt like I was facing another bereavement. When our child, or children, leave the nest, we encounter a massive void, even if there are still plenty of other little birds to feed and nurture. The fact is that a space has been created and only one person can fill it: our child that has moved on. But is there another way?

I have overcome the void I felt when my son left home by filling my nest with many different kinds of eggs. I don't want to hoard this information; I want to share, with you, what I feel I have been guided to write in these chapters.

Not long ago, I took myself on an *ayahuascan* journey in Madrid, and, through this experience, I had an epiphany to share my story with you. We live in a world shrouded in darkness, and it is up to us to shed light and make the world a brighter place.

In your hands, you have a workbook—to help guide *you,* my dear friend—to get back on your feet once your babies have flown your nest. Each chapter name came from a forum of *empty nesters.* If you are suffering, or maybe just not doing too good, you may not know how to move on. If that's the case, then I hope, that by following the steps in this book, you will find the strength to cope daily with the deafening silence and the empty dining room chairs. See you on the other side!

Love Kizzi x
mother of three

Chapter 1

EYES SWOLLEN SHUT

Your task is not to seek for love, but merely to seek and find all the barriers within yourself that you have built against it.

—Rumi

Nest Building

I HAVE THREE CHILDREN, AND THEY are all completely different. I like to think I have shared my love equally. It's not until you have a second child (or more) that you realise there is always plenty of love available, a never-ending pot, in fact. I didn't realise it was possible to love a person so much. I never really understood the meaning of *unconditional love* until I became a mother. There is an abundance of love.

When we came home from hospital with our firstborn, I stood in the doorway of our three-storey Victorian villa in East Sussex. I couldn't believe I was allowed to bring him home without a nurse, a midwife, or a manual. Underneath my flabby and scarred body, I was really scared. Dave, a passing neighbour and father of four, came by to congratulate us, commenting that we wouldn't get a good night's sleep for the next eighteen years. I thought he was joking.

I loved being a mum and couldn't wait to take my son out in my sister-in-law's second-hand, suspension-driven, Silver Cross perambulator, which I could never manage to get through shop doors. I soon hated that pram with a vengeance but had been informed it was simply the best—and what did I know about baby equipment? This was the start of my loss of control. Advice came from all directions and I became a headless chicken. Breastfeed him, bottle-feed him, burp him, leave him to cry, give him solids, give him molasses. And as for vaccinations. I just wanted to give him love. Eventually I was pushed too far and an altercation was to be had with my mother-in-law. I had made a stand and was stunned I had done this—in front of the entire family on a Sunday roast-dinner day as well! To be honest, I didn't feel great about that, but I had made the decision to bring my son up the way I felt was right, by following my maternal instincts and not those of an old-fashioned, interfering know-it-all. Looking back, I realise she was doing her best and giving me the advice that she had probably been given by her mother. But being a first-time mum puts us in a vulnerable position; it takes courage to hold our own. My advice is to listen to advice but not necessarily act on it, including this advice! Follow your instincts. That's what they're there for!

The friends I'd made at my antenatal yoga class were a lifeline in those early days. We would meet weekly with our babies, alternating at someone's house with a child minder, a yoga teacher, and a couple of bottles of vitamin B in the guise of red wine. I learned that little girl babies tended to be quieter and calmer and little boy babies were more active. But as they developed into crawlers and toddlers, they had elements of each other.

My son was not a good sleeper. It was not until he was eighteen months old that I got my first full night's kip. I wondered if that was what the neighbour had meant.

Because my first child had arrived in this world more or less on demand, I looked at my diary to 'organise' another baby. The hormones were certainly not being paid this time because it appeared I now had *second something infertility*. After nearly two years of chasing my husband round the mulberry bush, the kitchen table, and the bedroom, there was still no sign of baby number two. Falling back into the trap of following advice, I went to the doctor, who wanted to book me for treatment. The word *treatment* sent the hairs on the back of my neck in an upward direction, so I thought I'd sort something out myself.

We attended a special 'alternative' clinic and met a wonderful woman who took hair samples. My husband was, and still is, bald, so she sent him to the bathroom with a pair of scissors and a spoon! After a couple of weeks, our hair diagnoses informed us of nutrient deficiencies; I recall that zinc and selenium were the main culprits. We purchased the remedies and promised not to drink alcohol, tea, or coffee; plus, we had to eat lots of vegetables. Fingers crossed (but not legs!), we should become pregnant within three months. It took us two.

Our second son arrived on time. He was an elective caesarean due to my apparently small pelvic girdle and the emergency C-section I had delivering my firstborn, after a failed attempted home water birth. He was a wonderful, well-behaved child, full of love and enthusiasm, yet he was quite different from his older brother. We had tried very hard to bring him into our world, which could never be the same without him. He is loved equally, unconditionally and abundantly.

Eighteen months passed before we decided it was time to add a pink member to our growing family. I researched and discovered that if conception took place five days after the egg was released then it was more probable that a female addition would arrive, simply because the speedy male tadpoles start to die off, leaving the slower girlie ones to arrive just in time. And *voilà!* Pink Baby Number Three was born on 28 February. Our love flowed for all of our children continuously.

We often considered going for a fourth child, but, although I was sometimes headless, I was no longer a spring chicken, so we stopped—with immense gratitude for the gift of our three healthy and happy little people.

Nest Full

My children were my life. Alongside electing to be a stay-at-home mum, I had always earned my own living and whilst I had a lovely, supportive husband, I wanted to continue earning my own bread and butter. I started to build up a small property portfolio because in those days there were no buy-to-let schemes and the banks were corruptly generous in dishing out the dosh. This allowed me to work from home, in my own time, but be around for my children.

My husband was starting to be noticed in his world of business and began to devote a great deal of time building up his career. Many times I felt I was a single mother due to the days and nights he was away working and staying in hotels around the country. But I wasn't, of course. I was blessed with a husband and three perfect children.

Everything evolved around them: my work life, my social life, and my family life. There was Tumble Tots, Little Dippers, and Sing-a-Song-a-Susie, and I lost count of the visits to Drusillas Zoo. Oh yes, and my favourite: Middle Farm. That was when we started buying chickens. Then we got some orphaned lambs (fourteen of them), a cockerel, two Shetland ponies, two llamas, several hamsters, and three bearded dragons. Oops, I mustn't forget the fish. We already had the two cats before the children were born, although they fell out with each other once the babies took their places on my lap.

Life couldn't be any better. I was totally fulfilled as a mother. I could not imagine life any other way, and when my mother said that being a mum is the hardest job, I refused to give her the satisfaction of agreeing because, to me, it isn't a job. It is a vocation. At times, it is, perhaps, even a vacation, such as when I watched three little children in their matching red sweatshirts running off to the school gate together. And when they were all playing on the climbing frame in the garden. And making jewellery out of dried pasta. And …

'Best days of your life,' people would tell me. 'Enjoy them whilst you've got them,' said another. 'They're all yours at the moment, so make the most of it!' I was lost in my children.

A friend recently said to me that the problem with family life is when the mother sometimes falls *in* love with her children and *out of* love with her husband. I think that is a valid point for many of us. Sadly, in some circumstances, the husband appears to have fulfilled his role and is pushed aside. It's true enough in many of the animal species, but at least we don't eat our partners like the black widow spider!

But as much as I loved my role as mummy, like most, I was also very tired. Constantly. It wasn't always *Little House on the Prairie*.

My husband was away so much, I had a business to run, and we had moved from the city, now living in the country with our menagerie, which meant driving absolutely everywhere. There were no buses or trains, and I became a fishwife in the morning, screaming to get them ready for school. Then I returned home to clean the house, wash, shop, and cook, you know, before I was back to collect them again.

I'd go to bed exhausted and, at times, guiltily wished for them to hurry up and grow so they could start taking care of themselves. Be careful what you wish for, huh! One day I noticed I hadn't shouted at them in the morning for a couple of weeks. They were taking stock! They *were* growing up.

Nursery school, infant and junior, secondary, and then college. Where did all that go? I was forewarned that when they get to secondary school the time whizzes by, but hey! Hang on a sec—or a few more years, even. I take it back. Don't grow up!

But they do. They become involved with university, the forces, a backpack, or another woman in the guise of girlfriend (or boyfriend). All that work to be handed over to someone else.

My daughter's transformation was slightly different as I seemed to know what to look for, but it's also the hardest as she'll be the last one gone. I tried to read the signs as she evolved from cuddling me and *sharing* my mobile phone to getting her own. Then one day on holiday in Spain, she snatched it from me as I scrolled a photo too far. I was shocked and saddened, and my friend scolded me. But she didn't understand what I knew at that moment. I had lost my controllable child, and it was time to evolve with her. No longer my little baby girl, she was blossoming into my young best friend at a more grown-up level.

Only this week my daughter mentioned those wonderful childhood days and how she wished *she* could go back. She had been looking through old photographs, catching memories in her mind, *in full, vibrant colour,* and fantasising of a life with no responsibilities but simply frolicking in fields with family and friends and butterflies.

So it is not just Mum and Dad who experience the empty nest syndrome. It is a loss for all of us but made harder for the parents because we are not the ones leaving. We are not going off into the world to discover undiscovered things, yet to be discovered. However, *this doesn't have to be the case!* I repeat. This doesn't have to be the case. We *can* discover a great deal. I've done it! There is certainly no reason why you can't. It's all about the mindset. And filing. I'll come back to that later.

Finding my nest builder—it took time and experience!

When I was nineteen, my heart was broken. The breaker knows that now but I'm not sure he knew it thirty-five years ago. He was my first true love. I met him on a kibbutz in Israel when I was just nineteen. I'd gone off adventuring and fell *in love*. I was totally hooked, partly because he seemed very exciting with his guitar slung round his shoulder (that he couldn't play), long blond surfer hair, brown eyes, and an exotic foreign dialect. He knew his music, poetry, and prose, especially Bob Dylan. He quoted many lines to me, which I thought were his. I didn't care. He could spout anything to me; I was addicted. I followed him halfway round the world, and we backpacked for many months together, camping by rivers and waterfalls, getting stoned, and having fun. No responsibilities, no ties. Freedom. Then he followed me to the UK but got restless living under my parents' roof whilst swilling out pigs all day for a living. He went off adventuring again, this time to Europe, with a promise to return within six months.

One of the qualities I admire in people is honesty. I think that if you are honest and tell the truth, you don't trip up. He was honest when I sent him a letter and asked if he had met someone else on his trip. 'Yes' he wrote back.

There was a lot of to-ing and fro-ing whilst we tried to sort out this three-some business, but of course it wasn't going to work. He returned to me and one evening, I eavesdropped on a phone conversation, and, although I could only hear his answers, I easily worked out the questions. I grabbed his stuff and chucked it in a bin bag, threw it out the front door, and told him to fuck off. It was late at night but I didn't care. It felt good to say. My conservative father was aware of all these goings-on but continued to sit in his favourite armchair, smoking his pipe without comment. He had never heard me swear before because it was not allowed in our house. He was listening to me grow up.

I subsequently learned that the heartbreaker had an unplanned child

6

on the way. My heart shattered again. He was starting to build a nest whereas I thought he was an adventurer, like me.

I threw myself into work and saved money so I could travel more. I spent months backpacking through the US, travelling on a Trailways Bus overnight to cut hotel costs. I had a lot of adventures.

After spending time in Tahiti, I arrived in Australia, where I met Bruce (you're right, not his real name!) He had previously built a nest with Sheila in Sydney, but it hadn't worked. They had a beautiful daughter. After several months, I called my mum to say I was getting married and intended to live in Australia and would be a step-mum, but as soon as those words came out of my mouth, I knew it wasn't right for me. Down Under is a very long way from the UK in time, money, and distance. Bruce said he would be happy to come and live in the UK with me but needed time to tie up some loose ends and come to terms with leaving his child behind. In all honesty, I didn't give any consideration to his child. I had no experience of building a nest; I had only left one. We agreed that I would continue travelling and meet up in Sri Lanka in a couple of months. I wanted him to be sure that what he was doing was right for him.

I continued my journey through Asia with my newfound friend Jen. She was very sweet and we had a lot of fun together; however, having this fun made me realise I wasn't ready to build a nest. I wanted to keep adventuring. By myself. I told my fiancé this. He wasn't having any of it. I told him again. And again. I lost. The guilt started to take over because I knew he was leaving his daughter for me, so I went along with it but with great reluctance. Not a positive foundation for nest-building.

I greeted him at Colombo International Airport and immediately felt sick. I couldn't go through with this relationship. I told him again, and we argued and I thought that was the end of it. We went our separate ways in Sri Lanka, but a couple of weeks later, when I boarded the plane to return home, to my surprise and horror, he was already on it, a few rows behind me. Again, I felt sick.

We walked through arrivals together, and I put on a brave face for my parents. I hadn't seen my family for two years, and my 'fiancé' was not going to spoil it. He kept saying how much he was looking forward to spending 'Christmas with the in-laws'.

It never happened.

We rented a flat together, both got jobs, and tried to build our nest, but the foundation was just not right. I didn't love him. At a Christmas event we had a huge row, so big that I had to leave the party. He followed me and became physically aggressive. I was shocked but still, as stupid as it was, felt guilty about him leaving his daughter to be with me. It was obvious I didn't want to be with him. We just didn't fit. That night, when he followed me, he literally left me in the gutter, battered and bruised. I remember seeing people walk past me and could not believe this was happening. No one stopped to assist. Friends from the party came to find me and got me home, where I safely locked myself inside once they left.

In the early hours of the morning, he came home but he couldn't gain access. I told him to leave and stop waking up the neighbours. I called the police. Because he paid rent, they let him in. They had a quiet word with him, and he apologised for being loud and unsociable. They asked me if I would be happy for him to sleep on the sofa. I said no, but he paid half the rent so they said he could. He didn't sleep there of course. Once they had 'done their duty' and left, he did what he thought was his. And all hell broke loose.

I was violently raped that night and he left shortly after. I have never seen him since. I took my black eye to spend Christmas with my parents, and they were so gracious in accepting my story of me bumping into a door. They didn't even ask where he was. Down Under is certainly where he belonged.

No guilt is enough for tolerating mental or physical abuse, or rape, from anyone. Thank god I hadn't hatched any eggs with him. There's *always* an upside.

When we bring children into this world, they come with a huge responsibility. We are creating new human beings who will eventually take care of, not just themselves, but the human race and the entire planet, and it is our duty to teach them correctly. I wanted to make sure that the daddy in my nest was the right one, if there was such a being.

Filling your empty nest

I 'ran away' from home at seventeen. I backpacked around the world for over seven years, looking for fun, adventure, excitement, and ultimately, me. I now know that you do not have to go anywhere to find any of these things because they are all in one spot. And that is the very spot on which you are standing, right now. They are within your very being.

Having experienced the gaping hole in my heart when my first child left home, I learned to fill this void in ways which did not mean simply moving on or making a plan. The empty nest is about trying to find what you want to do with *your* life. You have been so busy managing everybody else's that when you pick up and look into a mirror, instead of a magnifying glass, it can be scary. Our children will always be there; they are living their lives as nature planned and, finally, are on their own. This is what we want for them. Now it is your time to live a happier and more productive life, in which these bittersweet feelings disappear so you can be fulfilled once again. You're filling that hole with purpose. Right?

Before we learn to do this, here's food for thought:

1. You are allowed to reinvent yourself, feel sad, and cry. I encourage you to do so.
2. You may at times become a little depressed or experience abandonment. The nights may be torture. You may get disgruntled, frustrated, and angry. No problem. All of this stuff is good because you are *being* a human not 'doing one'.
3. Maybe join a group or forum and then ask the members what they do to get by.
4. You could take a guess about what to do in your life next, a 50/50 choice of getting it right (like Who Wants to be a Millionnaire).
5. Or you could 'Phone A Friend' and I include myself in that option. Friends are great and there is no doubt we need sisters (and brothers) for this journey. People need other people to survive. Some of them will absolutely give you sound advice, as will I (if you want to take it!) With the help of this book, you'll

soon be laying different eggs that will hatch into happiness, positivity, and purpose.

So come with me, as I show you how *not* to hate going home, where you currently feel scared and powerless. We will work through this transition together and learn to have fun without the kids. This is your playground. You know the saying that what we reap is what we sow? I am going to help you sow the right seeds (or lay healthy new eggs) by making the right choices so that you can discover what it is costing you *not* to solve this problem. I've gone through the mill a few times myself, but I'm no longer as stale as I was. In fact, I like to see myself as a fresh, fluffy loaf to feed new birds with! And this time I get to choose which ones I feed.

> *When you're drowning, you don't say 'I would be incredibly pleased if someone would have the foresight to notice me drowning and come and help me,' you just scream.*
>
> —John Lennon

In the next chapter we help you realise that you truly are not alone in what you are experiencing. We will also start putting into practice ways to build a new nest.

Chapter 2

THOSE EMPTY BEDROOMS

When I was 5 years old, my mother always told me that happiness was the key to life. When I went to school, they asked me what I wanted to be when I grew up. I wrote down 'happy'. They told me I didn't understand the assignment, and I told them they didn't understand life.

—John Lennon

WELL, I'VE TOLD YOU A little about me, so now it's your turn. I get how you are feeling right now, and I also know you like to help people. Otherwise you wouldn't be reading this book. You may also be feeling lonely because those you used to help have left home or are about to.

Pause for thought here. Take a minute and think about what you have done in your life to help your children, besides giving them unconditional love. Most of the jobs you did were helpful (to them), but are there certain things that stick out in your mind that you *really enjoyed* doing? When they were little, did you like taking them to the park, perhaps meeting new people and chatting, or did you prefer to go to the swimming baths? Did you watch them swim or join in? Were you more comfortable making a mess on the kitchen table with *papier mache* or face painting? Driving them everywhere? Reading to them? What else comes to mind? Think of the things you have done with, and for, your children and what resonated with you the most. If you start to feel nostalgic, that's fine. Make a cup of tea and grab the photo album;

then relive those wonderful times *in vibrant colour* and start writing down the ones you enjoyed the most. Be sure you make the distinction here and ascertain the tasks you liked to do *for yourself* and not merely because you were spending time with your offspring. Don't rush. Try to list a good selection of five to ten projects you genuinely enjoyed—even if your children were not actively involved.

We're going to create another list now. Are there things you do currently, or could see yourself doing, to contribute to society whilst your children are in less need of your assistance? Do you volunteer your time to charities or organisations, contribute financially by donating to causes you believe in, keep an eye on an elderly neighbour, or offer advice to friends and family? Do you post positive comments on social media, perhaps also signing petitions to help change the world?

You can do this, you know: change the world. You can change yours. But you have to start at the beginning, which is by making a choice. *And this is where I come in. I'm going to help you with this.*

Feelings

Looking round your empty nest, having written your lists, what do you feel, and what comes to mind? These are two different questions. The first is about how your body feels—do you feel cold, warm, panicky? Are you breathing more quickly? Do you feel sad or sick, anxious, and stressed? Take stock and notice what is going on with your physical body; grab some paper and make notes.

What comes to mind and where is your mind/body when you feel this? Is it when you walk in the door at the sight of the perfectly tidy, empty bedroom? If you have a partner at home, does he know that you are sad but feels glad he has you all to himself again? Have you tried reconnecting with your spouse? Do you talk to each other? What else? Grab a coffee, sit down, and start to brainstorm. Do you feel selfish, lonely, like you can't cope? Do you have mixed emotions? Are you afraid of depression or are you already depressed?

Write it all down and then take a breath.

The first thing you need to know is that you are not alone. That's an important message, so I will repeat it slowly. You are not alone.

There, let it sink in. You may think this doesn't make any difference in the way you feel at the moment. It probably doesn't. But we are all connected and you need to know this.

When you drop a pebble into a small lake, the water ripples outward, eventually reaching the shore on all sides, connecting and affecting the entire lake. There is movement from that one small pebble. When you have an ache in your lower back, it may be caused by tension in your shoulders yet you feel the problem is to do with your lumbar spine. Our entire body is connected. What we do with our little finger will have some bearing on our big toe. Underneath our skin we have something called *myofascia*. Under a microscope fascia resembles a spiderweb or fishnet. It is very organised and very flexible when in a healthy state. It can best be described as a complete body suit which runs from the top of your head down to the bottom of your toes. A 'onesy'. It is continuous and has no beginning or end and can be found almost everywhere in your body. Like yarn in a sweater, the entire body is connected by the fascia. It is a continuous weave of material. And, like a pull or snag in a sweater, damage to an area of fascia can affect distant areas in your body, even years later. Remember these points for a moment.

Inside and Outside

When we have a negative thought, we may start to create a physical reaction, perhaps a shortness of breath or even a panic attack. However, we may not notice or be aware of the cause because we may not connect the bodily reaction to the thought that triggered it. From now on, though, if you want to get better, back to and beyond your normal, happy and healthy self, I suggest you make some notes.

I have wanted to write a book for a long time—over thirty years, in fact—but the time was never right. There were too many toos; too busy, too tired, too clueless, etc. There was always something else to do, a family to feed, or someone in the way. Plenty of distractions.

I recently had a social lunch with my solicitor, and, inevitably, we got to talking about my book. I casually checked with him whether or not I could put authentic names in without getting into trouble. Whilst chatting, I became aware of why this was the right time to write my book and why I had asked the question. It was because my mother has just died. As painful as that is, now that both my parents have moved on to a greater plane, I am able to experience freedom. This is the upside of being a mature orphan. I can now talk openly about things I would not have wanted my parents to know should they pick up a copy of what you are holding. It would be too painful for them to hear about my rape, for instance. It would have been too painful for me to write it whilst they were still alive. Now, my mind, body, and soul are more relaxed.

So this takes us back to honesty. I could not write a self-help book if I were not telling the absolute truth, which brings us to your list of physical sensations and any connected thoughts. Find yourself a notebook and keep it with you. When you find you are challenged, feeling useless and heartbroken, write down any physical sensations that arise. When you glance at a favourite unused egg cup, notice what thoughts come to mind. After you have done this for a couple of days, take it one step further and write down whatever comes to mind when I ask you what is *most challenging* about your empty nest?

Our whole life is a game of Monopoly, starting and stopping and meeting challenges on the way. But quite often we are too busy to notice what is happening, and we just plough through. So I am asking you to slow down. Be open to what is around you.

A lot of what I have to share with you is about going within. Remember chapter 1, when I mentioned you can have adventure on one spot, without going anywhere? I'm not talking about being introspective here, and we also need to choose our moment, but this is where the happiness resides. *Inside.*

Of course there are times to be open, to see what's around you, what message the universe is sending. Before I started this book, I asked for some signs from the universe, and maybe this book that you're holding is one of your signs—*my* message to *you.* Open your eyes and see what is being presented to you.

A student of mine came to me recently with tears in her eyes because she could relate to the particular yoga class I had been teaching that week; we were working on the heart *chakra.* I will discuss the chakra system in a later chapter, but for now try to understand that a chakra is a wheel of energy to the front and back of your body. If we have it in balance, then *we* are in balance regarding that particular aspect of our being. Most of us aren't, I must add, but that is why we roam the planet—to learn to be in balance and live in harmony.

This student explained that as much as she gave to them and did for her sons, it was never enough, and she felt useless and heartbroken. She was also concerned about the relationship between her youngest son and her husband, and she felt at a loss. I reminded her that the relationship with which she needed to be concerned was *the one she had with herself.* If she was being truthful to herself, then everything else would fall into place; the relationship she had with her sons, as well as the relationships they had with their individual parents and with each other. And of course, the relationship they had with themselves. After a few reassuring words, the tears dissipated, and within a few minutes we ended up doing a little Irish jig together (it was St Patrick's Day!) Obviously, more work needs to be done, but this was a start.

We cannot control the relationships that other people have, even if we think we can. We can, however, become very upset and hurt by them, which is not good. But this is in *our* control. When we seek power and try to control people, we waste energy, so we must learn to accept this, let go, and control ourselves instead. Doing this, we will accomplish more.

Remember the ripple effect with the pebble and the lake. You are that pebble. That's all you need to be. You don't have to be a pink pebble or a big pebble, a happy or sad pebble. You don't have to always make the beach look pretty, and you aren't responsible for making the sun shine. You are just a pebble in true congruity and integrity. By being that pebble and dropping into the lake, you will affect everything around you, simply by being yourself and nothing else. You are connected. And the same goes for other pebbles that are also dropped into the lake; they will affect you. **Be true to yourself, and who you are.** The rest will fall into place without your worry, concern, control, or interference. We are all connected in ways our human brain does not always understand, and there are things we are not able to change as much as we may like to. Allowing people to also be themselves, whether we like what that person is doing and how that person is reacting to another *is not our business.* It is better that we simply observe and carry on being our true selves, without judgement. Tricky, huh? Like the monk. We must learn to be that simple, strong, and solid pebble that has no concern in making the beach look beautiful or the waves fall upon the shore. None of that is our business. We must concentrate on being a pebble, and it is as simple as that. Emotions do crop up because that is what is important: to feel and experience life. And not every aspect of life is fun and happy.

When my mother died, I started to look for a sign that she had crossed over happily and had rejoined my father. I chose to look for stars, as this was what we both looked for when my father died (along with feathers). Stars appeared in the most obscure places, and I find warmth and comfort in this sign from the universe and from my mother. When my father died, I asked for a sign from the other side, and I chose this to be a white feather. I still use this connection between our two worlds and place my feathers in a sacred jar in my office. They offer me reassurance and a connection with my lovely dad; for whatever reason, they've helped me a lot.

Julian Lennon had a similar belief and has built a whole foundation from this.

> Dad once said to me, that should he pass away, if there was some way of letting me know he was going to be ok – that we were all going to be ok – the message would come to me in the form of a White Feather. Then something happened to me, whilst on tour with the album, Photograph Smile, in Australia. I was presented with a White Feather by an Aboriginal tribal elder, from The Morning People, which definitely took my breath away.
>
> The White Feather Foundation was created for the purpose of giving a voice and support to those who cannot be heard. The tribal elders asked for my help, as I could bring awareness to their plight and to others who were suffering the same. Having had the White Feather bestowed upon me, I knew this endeavour was to be part of my destiny. One thing for sure is that the

White Feather has always represented peace to me, as well as communication ...

—Julian Lennon, 2009

So now you have your list and are starting to observe your mind and body. I suggest that you start externalising this exercise and look for signs in your daily life to see if anything shows up that may be part of your destiny.

I used to work for a recruitment agency in my twenties, and my boss had weekly meetings, during which she would remind us to search for new companies on our way to work. I wasn't involved in sales, but I became very observant through this experience and am always looking out for signs on buses, billboards, in fact, simply everywhere! On a trip to London this week, whilst considering research for this book, these are the messages that the universe sent my way. This was during a ninety-minute journey although I put them in my chosen order below. How does your mind interpret them? (My glass is always half full, by the way. Is yours?)

- Walls closing in
- Do not take any risks
- In an emergency, it is safer to stay on the train
- Use the red button to alert the driver (Who is the driver in your life?)
- Follow instructions from staff or emergency services—southbound down, northbound up (Which way do you want to go?)
- Items trapped in doors cause delays (What are your items?)
- Press to operate lift (Who is the operator?)
- The stairway has 136 steps, use in an emergency (this is only chapter 2, your second step!)
- Help Point, Fire, Alarm, Emergency, Information
- Way out
- From a leap to a step

- Looking for your next job, search find, apply (although parenting will always be your most important job!)
- Chop and Change (hairdressers)
- *The Navigator* (new album)
- Every journey matters—London Underground
- "We must not lose our facility to dare, particularly in dark days." —Winston Churchill (on a billboard)

I found the next message especially interesting. This shop is an upmarket department store.

- Heal and Son (appropriate for the empty-nesters with boys). This was located next to a lesser-known shop called:
- Dwell (and both were opposite a pub called …)
- The Hope (Fitzrovia)
- *The Penny Has Finally Dropped* (This was a new play about to open, and a perfect message—perfect timing!)
- Good Vibes (health studio)
- Xlerator (hand-drying machine in toilet)
- Rising Sun Public House (I'm thinking of my boy leaving the nest here and moving up in the world.)
- Starbucks (successful young sons, at that)
- Waitrose (supermarket—Do I want her to stay at home?)
- Well done mum, I've turned out awesome (an advert for mother's day cards)
- Life is out there (motto on a person's shopping bag)
- We are what we do (National Westminster Bank)

And finally on the way home:

- The first step is to take one

So give it a go; it can be a lot of fun and very insightful!

I was driving in town and noticed a friend still driving her teenagers to school. Teenage. My initial response was, 'How crazy! Why don't they get the bus like all the others?' But then I remembered her story.

She is from Croatia, and several years ago she'd been living in Poland with her new husband and two four-year-old sons. They were bound for the UK to start a new life with her ten-year-old daughter from a previous marriage. Within minutes of arriving at the airport, her ex-husband appeared, holding a legal document stating that she could not take their daughter out of the country. She had to make a decision there and then. She decided and got on the plane with her new family, whilst her daughter still lives in Poland. *Sophie's Choice.* As I watched her car drive passed, I understood why she doesn't let those children out of her sight. But one day, I feel she may be in need of the messages in this book.

Having opened my mind to the universe for signs, I needed to jot the messages down. After seeing her, I told myself to get a notebook. When I got home, it was already there. My backpacking son had sent one from Thailand as a late birthday present. Thank you, William. Thank you, Universe.

I truly see these signs as messages from the cosmos. The famous psychologist Carl Jung coined the word *synchronicity* as he believed there was no such thing as coincidence. In his book *Synchronicity* (1952), Jung tells the following story as an example of a synchronistic event:

> My example concerns a young woman patient who, in spite of efforts made on both sides, proved to be psychologically inaccessible. The difficulty lay in the fact that she always knew better about everything. Her excellent education had provided her with a weapon ideally suited to this purpose, namely a highly polished Cartesian rationalism with an impeccably "geometrical" idea of reality. After several fruitless attempts to sweeten her rationalism with a somewhat more human understanding, I had to confine myself to the hope that something unexpected and irrational would turn up, something that would burst the intellectual retort into which she had sealed herself. Well, I was sitting opposite her one day, with my back to the window, listening to her flow of rhetoric. She had an impressive dream the night before, in which someone had given her a golden scarab – a costly piece of jewellery.

While she was still telling me this dream, I heard something behind me gently tapping on the window. I turned round and saw that it was a fairly large flying insect that was knocking against the window-pane from outside in the obvious effort to get into the dark room. This seemed to me very strange. I opened the window immediately and caught the insect in the air as it flew in. It was a scarabaeid beetle, or common rose-chafer (*Cetonia aurata*), whose gold-green colour most nearly resembles that of a golden scarab. I handed the beetle to my patient with the words, "Here is your scarab." This experience punctured the desired hole in her rationalism and broke the ice of her intellectual resistance. The treatment could now be continued with satisfactory results.

—Carl Jung

Be open to the signs!

Do you know the following story?

A fellow was stuck on his rooftop in a flood. He was praying to God for help. Soon a man in a rowing boat came by and the fellow shouted to the man on the roof. 'Jump in, I can save you.' The stranded fellow shouted back. 'No, it's OK. I'm praying to God and he is going to save me.' So the rowing boat went on. Then a motorboat came by. The fellow in the motorboat shouted, 'Jump in, I can save you!' To this, the stranded man said, 'No thanks, I'm praying to God and he is going to save me. I have faith.' So the motorboat went on. Then a helicopter came by and the pilot shouted down, 'Grab this rope and I will lift you to safety.' To this the stranded man again replied, 'No thanks. I'm praying to God and he is going to save me. I have faith.' So the helicopter reluctantly flew away.

Soon the water rose above the rooftop and the man drowned. He went to Heaven. He finally got his chance to discuss this whole situation with God, at which point he exclaimed, 'I had faith in you but you didn't save me! You let me drown. I don't understand why!' To this God replied, 'I sent you a rowing boat and a motorboat and a helicopter. What more did you expect?'

Take notice of the signs that land on your path! It's like practising yoga. We have to shift our vision as we can't always see where the pose is taking us as we stretch, balance, crawl, fall and bump into things in our postures. And like reading braille. We can't see what is underneath so we have to learn to feel our way around. We all do this, trying to find our way in life, so don't ever think you are alone on this path—you are not!

Things to-do list:

1. Buy a beautiful journal. Spend time in selecting this with a special pen to go alongside.
2. Take yourself and your new journal out to a pond, lake, or even a large puddle. Throw in a pebble and watch the ripple effect.
3. Reflect on the activities you most enjoyed with your children when they were younger. Scribble notes and sketch pictures.
4. See what comes up for you as you become aware of your physical feelings and thoughts, and make notes.
5. Start to notice the signs the universe is offering. Jot them down, and join any dots that become obvious, any messages that make sense.
6. Keep journaling about any differences you notice in your lifestyle, feelings, or habits.

In the next chapter, you will learn that there is a way out of this for you and a future to be had. Read on!

Chapter 3

I FEEL LIKE I CAN'T BREATHE

Here is the test to find whether your mission on Earth is finished: if you're alive, it isn't.

—Richard Bach

ARE YOU DESPERATELY SEEKING 'SUCCOURANCE', the act of seeking out affectionate care and social support? Well, you're in the right place, and there are two ways we can address this. I can hold your hand as we walk together; I will be your prop. Or we can walk side by side, and I will be your friend instead. Let's aim for the second option, but I will hold your hand—and even carry you—until you are ready to stand in *tadasana*, as solid as a mountain.

Have you heard of this little Chinese proverb: *Give a man a fish, you feed him for a day. Teach a man to fish and you will feed him for a lifetime.* Today I'm going to teach you to fish! We won't need a fishing rod where we are going, but I want to show you that there is a way out from the life that you find so hard at times.

You may have worked out by now that one of the hats I wear is that of a yoga teacher. I am not particularly bendy, and I was certainly not a gymnast or a professional dancer. I could never do handstands and cartwheels at school, so I'm not that fussed that I can't do them now. Some schools of yoga expect you to do all that sort of stuff, but that's not where I'm coming from. Yoga is actually a science and a way of living; it's not just about looking cool and fit on a mat. It's about being in balance, in harmony, with yourself and finding peace. The word *yoga* means to unite, to yoke together.

I teach my lovely students different aspects of yoga which incorporate breath awareness, relaxation, and most importantly *ahimsa,* which means being kind to yourself. I remind everyone at the end of the class to do this, to pat themselves on the back for taking time to come out to class—rain, wind, or shine—dedicating ninety minutes to themselves with kindness and "non-violence". That is what *ahimsa* means in *sanskrit,* "non-violence". We don't compete in our class, even with ourselves, and we don't worry about what our neighbours are doing on the mat next to us. In fact, sometimes we have a real laugh, and on the odd occasion I swear, which is not good teaching (as my children remind me). The cabin crew on board an aeroplane teach us *ahimsa* when they tell us to put on our own oxygen mask first in case of emergency.

What to do in the evenings (or mornings, or afternoons)

A lot of the feelings we have create stress. In fact, did you know that most illness is caused by stress? When I researched my paper on this subject for my yoga teacher training diploma, I was fascinated at what I learned—how our mind controls our body and what we could do to change it to improve our health. Here's some information from my essay about stress you may find interesting.

Stress is a natural process of being human, a demand on the physical or mental energy which may exceed the resources available to cope with it, putting pressure on the body. It can have either a positive effect, creating excitement with an adrenalin rush empowering us to succeed, or it can become a negative entity, creating worry, suffering, and ultimately disease or illness. Stress can be external (from the environment or social situations) or internal (illness, medical procedure, worry).

Everyone has different stress levels. A situation that is intolerable to one person may stimulate another. How we feel is determined not just by events and changes in the outside world, but by how we perceive and respond to them. Sometimes, we become very scared. Fear causes stress, as does change, and I believe that fear is simply a thought, something that pops into our mind and quite often stays there. It is a feeling that something may happen or fail to happen, but ultimately, it is just a thought which creates emotions. With your permission, those emotions turn into stress.

Stress is an inevitable part of life, and there are many things which we have little or no control over. Nevertheless, we do not have to be victims to stress; we can learn and grow from it.

Stress can initiate physiological responses known as the 'fight or flight' response, caused by the release of certain hormones when danger is sensed. The body may react in many ways—shortness of breath, slowing down the digestive system, heart palpitations, dilation of blood vessels, relaxation of the bladder, etc. Negative long-term unhealthy levels of stress cause anxiety, sleeplessness, high blood pressure, diabetes, and even cancer, to name but a few.

The fight or flight response was first noted by one of the early pioneers in stress research, Walter Cannon. In 1932 he established that when an organism experiences a shock or perceives a threat, it quickly releases hormones that help it to survive. *We* are organisms, so when we put ourselves in the fight or flight mode, we become anxious and jumpy, perhaps even aggressive and irritable. This may affect our ability to work or concentrate as our body has gone into survival mode, with the added possibility of making imbalanced decisions.

> Become aware of your breathing. Feel the air flowing in and out of your body. Feel your inner energy field. All that you ever have to deal with, cope with, in real life – as opposed to imaginary mind projections – is this moment. Ask yourself what "problem" you have right now, not next year, tomorrow or five minutes from now. What is wrong with this moment?
>
> —Eckhart Tolle

We can be fearful and stressed by virtually anything in life, such as simply crossing the road or watching a young child cross for the first time, by himself. We can become very stressed when our children leave home and we have to face a life without seeing them every day. This can make us feel angry, rejected, hurt, and unable to move on.

Other causes of stress include separation from a partner or the loss of a job and perhaps the fear of not having enough: enough money, enough food, enough time. Here you may feel selfish, alone, even crazy. In fact, any change in life's circumstances can cause an element of stress, whether the circumstance is real or in the imagination.

Adrenaline and cortisol are present in the body all the time, but levels increase in response to danger and stress. In the beginning, the effects are positive to help cope with any immediate danger, but long-term stress means cortisol builds up so the body becomes cortisol dominant, thereby creating a number of stress-related health problems. These can affect our learning, memory, and even our attention span. We become pale and sweat more, our mouth gets dry, and our digestive system closes down, thereby causing nausea and possibly vomiting. Instinct takes over from rational thought and reasoning. Have you experienced any of these sensations?

Stress affects our health in various ways, particularly chronic stress, which continues over long periods of time. It can lower our immune system so we're generally more susceptible to becoming ill. It can lead to high blood pressure and heart disease, everyday aches and pains, weight gain, sleep loss, lowering of sex drive, and skin conditions like psoriasis, hives, or eczema. Amazing, don't you think?

> *When you are under the strong emotional influences of fear,*
> *anger or even excessive joy, your body is out of balance, too.*
> *The stress of sudden joy can cause a heart attack just as easily*
> *as the stress of sudden rage.*

—Andreas Moritz

So what to do about it

Stress-reduction strategies, such as meditation, exercising, and relaxation, have been shown to reverse the negative effects of stress on our health by increasing endorphins and making more infection-fighting cells to boost our immune systems.

On another level, stress is also linked to attachment, the possession of material objects or the desire to possess something or someone. When we own something, we sometimes worry about losing it, and the thought of losing it can make us worry and feel stressed. So imagine what our body is doing when we think about our babies leaving home or when we feel our son or daughter has been taken from us. Some words of wisdom state that 'there is no ultimate benefit in making the material body comfortable at the expense of forgetting the prime necessity of life, which is to regain our loss of spiritual identity. The boat of human life is constructed in such a way that it must move toward a spiritual destination. Unfortunately, this body is anchored to mundane consciousness by five strong chains which are attachment' (His Divine Grace A. C Bhaktivedanta Swami Prabhupada, *The Science of Realisation*).

In yoga, the attachments are classed as

- the material body;
- kinsmen;
- land of birth and material possessions;
- science and religious forms; and
- holy rituals.

The less we are attached to, the less we have to worry about. Simple, huh? (Not really! It's a lifetime's work, probably many lifetimes).

Positively speaking, the *short-term* effects of stress include decreased sensitivity to pain, increased immunity, and heightened memory. Necessary stress in life is a good thing, as it spurs us on and encourages us to strive for something. Positive stress can make us ambitious and hard-working, helping us to become good achievers, but this needs to be monitored to ensure it doesn't tip out of balance. If we become too worried or fearful, we then become over stressed. Managing stress is about managing balance in one's lifestyle.

Dr Robert E. Svoboda states in his book *Prakriti* that 'structure in life helps reduce the effects of stress. Stress, or rather improper reaction to stress, creates new diseases and worsens pre-existent ones. Stress permits alien beings like viruses and cancerous cells to colonise new territory by impairing the immune system's ability to respond to invasion … no-one is immune from exposure to all stress, but we can improve our immunity to the stresses we do encounter'.

So we know now that stress occurs every time we have to adapt to a new situation. Every time our surroundings (physical, mental, emotional, social, and spiritual circumstances) change, we must change along with them and develop a new balance.

Before I reached forty, I wanted a classic Mercedes sports car, open top and bright red, so I was very fortunate to receive, from my lovely husband, this second-hand classic car on my fortieth birthday. It even had a huge blue satin ribbon wrapped round it. (Before I got to fifty, I had wanted to practice a headstand. It was a major achievement for me, especially because I could see the world from upside down and *in balance*. I have even greater aspirations before I reach sixty!) When I received the car, I was very happy, but I never saw it as a status symbol; it was just a car that I had always set my dreams on. It wasn't even very expensive, but I loved it and still do. Fifteen years on and she still sits proudly on my drive, satin ribbon in the glove compartment. The headstand was more about achieving something for myself, inwardly. It was about releasing my fears. After all, the only thing that could go wrong was that I would fall down, which I did several times, but I don't worry about that anymore because I have experienced the fear. Now there isn't any (well, maybe a bit!). **Your true self (soul) is immune to criticism and is unafraid of any challenge**.

> *Let me assert my firm belief that the only thing we have to fear is fear itself—nameless, unreasoning, unjustified terror.*
>
> —Franklin D Roosevelt

Deep relaxation and the benefits of relaxation techniques

In the 1970s a Harvard professor of medicine, Herbert Benson, claimed that the body could obtain the opposite feeling of stress by getting into a relaxed state, which he called the Relaxation Response. The Benson-Henry Institute for Mind Body Medicine at Massachusetts General Hospital teaches patients ways to counteract stress and build resiliency by eliciting the Relaxation Response. This is induced when one is in a deep state of rest, which is linked to decreased heart and breathing rates, lower blood pressure, relaxed muscle tension, the slowing of the metabolism, and a decrease in oxygen taken in. Not surprisingly, thinking becomes less active. If this is practised daily for approximately twenty minutes, the relaxation response will help increase energy, improve concentration, and extend memory, thereby keeping the body young.

Relaxation is a state of healing which rests the mind, allowing the body to rebalance, removing tension and stress, and rest at a very deep level. Energy is drawn in, allowing your parasympathetic nervous system to operate fully, slowing the heart, and narrowing the airways so your body's healing responds by removing external interference caused by stress.

Relaxation helps to maintain a healthy and balanced nervous system which will respond positively. The calmer your mind is, the deeper your body can relax.

By practising yoga (or something similar) we incorporate breathing and relaxation techniques, providing the opportunity to switch off the mind and live in the present moment. This removes any tension and stress from the body. You can start by practising with breath-work, such as the three-sector breath (chapter 7) or simply by watching and being aware of how you breathe. You can use sound or words to create a mantra as well as progressive relaxation, which helps us stay focused and brings our mind back to the practice if we become distracted.

Have strength and inner guidance in all you take on, for yourself and the multitude around you. Feel the weight of their plight, their interests and their hopes. And set upon your own path, with freedom to ride high and far from glory, and into the shadow of your own worldly existence. Have strength and courage to persevere in this nether region of selfhood, for it is here that we learn the ultimate secrets of hope and prosperity, and reap from within the charitable chaste state of Grace.

—Hercules, channelled on April 14, 2001

In chapter 2, we made lists of things we used to love doing with our children. Now we need to take a look at our lists and decide what we like the best from those childhood activities. Then we are going to find time in our schedule to get back to them.

Yoga was definitely at the top of my list. I see the benefits and chose to become a teacher, firstly, to make myself practice more often but subsequently, to share this amazing tool with whoever turns up in my class. I really feel as if I serve others when I teach my classes, workshops, or retreats. I remember many years ago I turned up to Sally's class and she wasn't there, so I burst out crying! You never know what you've got till it's gone, I think the song goes. Until then I had never realised how much I benefitted from the practice on a deep emotional and spiritual level, not just a physical one.

So, looking at your list of activities, what jumps out at you the most? You may have to adapt this. If you loved doing crafts with your children, how could you adapt that to fit in your life now? Would this be painting, drawing, card-making? If you loved story-telling, consider taking this further by starting to write regularly, maybe journaling, blogging, writing for a local charity magazine, or something along those lines. Who could your audience be? Visiting schools, hospitals, children's homes to read to people in need? If you liked making cakes with the kids, what about taking your cooking to another level by baking for the homeless, hospices, nursing homes, or local clubs. Can you see where these doors may open for you? Can you see how your body will react differently when you use it for a positive purpose and service to others? Because you don't have to just read, write, and bake: You can take your skills and creativity out into the world and share them with others. Feel the connection that is already there. This will not only keep you positive in mind, body, and spirit, but it also shows that you still have love to give and that this love is being given back to the universe, where we are all connected. Here are some other suggestions:

- Singing—join/start a choir and visit hospitals and old people's homes or children's homes
- Cooking—make cakes and curries for the homeless, the elderly, the lonely neighbour
- Writing—develop short stories, poetry, or articles and post them online; read them in children's wards
- Dancing—join/start a dance club and arrange an evening out for everybody once a month
- Walking—offer to take someone's dog out if they work all day, find lonely people
- Talking—join a local discussion/debating group or have a go at improvisation
- Pretending—join an amateur dramatic club and work in front of the audience or behind the scenes; attend an 'impro comedy' class
- Organising—arrange a charity dinner, dance, or auction
- Travelling—volunteer abroad for so many causes

Whatever your passion is, there is a way to bring out the best in you. When you ask yourself what you should do next that is most helpful, well, you will have the answer.

> *No one is useless in this world who lightens the burdens of another.*
>
> —Charles Dickens

They say it takes three months to create a new habit and three weeks to lose it, so stick with this new regime as much as you possibly can. You just need to commit for twelve weeks to something that you enjoy and that will make you de-stress. I call my yoga classes 'Stretch to De-stress,' and that is the main purpose of the ninety minutes. It doesn't involve full-on posture work; we have a session on breath awareness and chanting and a lovely ten minutes of deep relaxation at the end. The main reason that yoga is practised is to help us sit in meditation for a long time, but in the Western world, for many, it has been turned into a New Age aerobics! There are so many crazy styles of yoga, it's gone bonkers (and way too commercial!).

So, having found your favourite activity, see if there is also a relaxation class to get involved in, perhaps something you've not tried before. If yoga isn't your cup of tea, there are so many other options out there (I guess because there are so many of us needing support whilst feeling empty). How about a course on mindfulness, Tai Chi, chanting, singing, drumming, Qi Gong, meditation, or even taking regular time out to walk in nature? I urge you to find a class or activity that fits your schedule, which will help you through the tough times. This will encourage you to find a way to go on, I promise.

> When you are inspired by some great purpose, some extraordinary project, all of your thoughts break their bonds. Your mind transcends limitations; your consciousness expands in every direction; and you find yourself in a new, great and wonderful world. Dormant forces, faculties and talents become alive and you discover yourself to be a greater person than you ever dreamed yourself to be.
>
> —Patanjali

Things to-do list:

1. Choose a favourite activity from your list and put the wheels in motion.
2. Using your new-found passion, see where you can be in service to others.
3. Find another form of relaxation to try, something totally new to you.
4. What is your greatest fear and do you want to try to tackle it.

5. List five things you would love to try if there was absolutely nothing stopping you.

In the next chapter, we will look at our power system by working with the chakras and their colours. We will also learn how to take control by saying no!

Chapter 4

LEARNING *NOT* TO ALWAYS HELP

You don't need anybody to tell you who you are or what you are. You are what you are!

—John Lennon

I WAS A PARTY GIRL. WHEN I was thirteen, I used to get into all the eighteen-plus nightclubs, apart from Sherries. That was the only one that could see through me. I think it was because of my white ankle socks, which I thought looked trendy. My sister advised me to bide my time, to hold something back for when I was eighteen, but by seventeen I'd gone. I'd run away from home.

Years later I had to write that down once in an essay, that I'd run away, and my teacher commented, 'Well done'. I thought she was being sarcastic but she wasn't. And when I was asked at a job interview what was the bravest/scariest/worst/best/naughtiest/put your word here-est thing I'd ever done, this spouted from my mouth, and my potential boss said, 'Well done'.

My dad didn't think so. He washed his hands of me, or so my mum said. He'd lost control and I was the last one to leave the nest, so I guess he was hurting. What did I know? What did I care? The teenage years are selfish. With my own children, I could only watch, stand by, and be prepared to pick them up when they stumbled. I guess that's what my folks were doing, when I let them.

I remember sitting in the rear seat of a police car looking at the back of my son's head on one particular occasion. They had caught him smoking dope after climbing over the school fence. What goes around comes around, I guess. When I ran away, my destination was quite exotic. I flew off to Tenerife, one of the Canary Islands. I had everything planned, from putting myself on the contraceptive pill to booking a taxi in the early morning to pick me up at the end of the road so as not to disturb the neighbours (or my dad).

My god, what adventures I had. They would take up the entire book if I told them in detail. In a nutshell, after five months, I was deported, with two assertive policemen escorting me either side at the airport. With humiliation, I had to carry my own heavy suitcases. I wasn't allowed back into Spain for three years, according to my passport.

I had been living there illegally, working there illegally, and hanging out with drug dealers, obviously illegally. I didn't know they were dealers. I was also working alongside ladies of the night. I knew what they were, but I did say *alongside*. We worked in bars with a red light above the door and several curtained-off areas. So, when I sit in the back of a police car protecting one of my children, I can't blame him for experimenting, experiencing, and living his life. I just hope that ultimately he heads north and not south—remember the signs from the first chapter?

I ran away from home because, as much as I loved my dad, he was very controlling. He was a successful bank manager. On one occasion he asked my mum if she liked the patterned green wallpaper he'd chosen for the new branch he was managing.

'Yes, dear, very nice.'

'Good,' he said, 'I've ordered it for our lounge at home.' None of us liked it.

My mum was a warrior. 'Wonder Woman', strong, stubborn, selfless, and kind. She was from Liverpool. My dad was from South East London and was strong, stubborn, selfish, yet kind. He loved us all very much—me and my older brother and sister—but he couldn't quite let us be the people we were destined to be. I see this in many families now. I see parents sacrifice much of their hard-earned income to support their children through private education, university, and the like so that these young adults can follow the path their parents had intended for them.

I am very impressed with my friends son, a bright, A star student who disobeyed the rules by following his own. He was brilliant at school but didn't always enjoy it and got into trouble on several occasions, once for showing video clips on the computer of a man doing strange things with a fish. He could have talked his way out of that one, but he chose not to, as he didn't like the system. Instead of becoming the doctor or engineer that could have been his destiny, he chose to go into cage fighting and went off to Asia to train hard. I admire him so much because he followed his own path even though it was against all odds. I know he will go far, and, once he settles down, all that academia, that strength of character, that muddled intelligence, will serve him well. But on his own terms.

This is another aspect of empty nesting: watching our offspring disappear into the sunset doing things we aren't so sure about. It's hard to let go, but it's their journey and not ours. Their learning experience, not ours.

Of course, we are not only controlled by parents and elders (if we allow ourselves to be). We are controlled by the system, by authority, by the people in uniform (whatever that uniform may be), and I will talk more about that in chapter 6.

This chapter is about learning to say 'no', which is a very important life skill to have. When my dad told me I was too young to travel to Tenerife on my own, he was legally right, but something inside me was so strong. Prior to this dream, having left school at 16, I held down a very reliable 9–5 job in a bank, which I quite enjoyed. But imagine the adventures I'd have missed out on if I'd agreed with my dad because of what he wanted or because of his own fears (for me). Isn't this what life is about, following our own intimate journey rather than what someone sets out for us? But of course, letting go is hard to do.

So, is there anything now that you wish you could have done? Is there anything you may regret when you lie on your deathbed, anything you would do differently? You do realise that it is never too late, don't you? That the thing you always wanted to do is available to you now, even if it may have to be watered down a little. Have a think.

Fear is stupid. So are regrets.

—Marilyn Monroe

You have already made a list of things that you enjoy doing, so let's take it further to see what the big one is, what you really want to do. You are probably in a better place than ever to complete this task. You have no young children to hold you back. You have management skills from running a home and raising a family. You have life experience and you are not too old. You are never too old. You may have a spouse that thinks you're a little crazy, but he/she may also have a fantasy or regrets that need to be fulfilled, perhaps even joining you on yours!

Energy bodies (chakras)

I mentioned the *chakra* system earlier. I will explain what this is so that you know what I'm talking about. We are made of skin and bone, which forms our physical body. But there is also an energy body the untrained eye cannot see, which surrounds us. We sometimes call this the aura or *prana* or energy field. There are different names from different belief systems, and it doesn't matter what it is called as long as you have an understanding of what it is.

Do you ever get a feeling of someone being too close, in your space, even though they may not be touching you? Or a physical sensation if someone gives you the creeps, even though you may not have said one word? You are simply picking up on their energy field, their aura.

Within the aura there are seven main wheels of light that spin to the front and back of your physical body pulling in the energy that surrounds us all. Each *chakra* or energy wheel serves a different purpose and corresponds to the various parts of our body, depending where it is located.

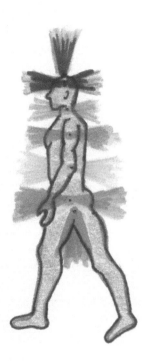

The root chakra is located at the base of the spine and promotes physical survival, vitality, stability, patience, courage, and material success. It gives us life force and natural instincts, and it connects us to the earth. To the trained eye, it is red in colour. If it is out of balance, we may feel ungrounded, scatty, or perhaps light-headed. Or we may feel heavy, lethargic, and overweight. If we could balance our root chakra, we would become stable and strong. Body parts associated are the coccyx, anus, large intestine, adrenal glands, back leg, feet and bones. The sound associated with the root is the note C.

The chakra at the top of our head is called the crown chakra, and, to the trained eye, is white or purple, which is very spiritual and sometimes 'religious'. It connects us with our own spirituality and whatever goes on above us (be it the universe, heaven, source, cosmos, or your own interpretation of god). I like to think of an older person with healthy white hair having a balanced crown chakra. They earned that privilege and wisdom. We practice meditation to find the stillness, awareness, understanding, and grace to achieve balance here. When out of balance, we become disconnected, cynical, and materialistic or perhaps overly intellectual with a spiritual addiction. We may also feel spaced out. The body parts connected to this area are the head, brain, and nervous system. The crown chakra promotes positive thought patterns, inspiration, and imagination. It constantly channels life energy into our system and aligns and balances all other chakras. It is in charge of our spiritual well-being, our connection to the higher self. The sound associated is B.

> *Perhaps we shall learn, as we pass through this age, that the 'other self' is more powerful than the physical self we see when we look into a mirror.*

> —Napolean Hill (Think and Grow Rich)

In the middle we have the green heart chakra, referred to as a 'bridge' because it connects the lower (self) chakras with those of the higher self, above the heart. When we have blockages here, and we all do, then we become more self protecting, needing guidance and support. Perhaps we have a fear of intimacy or become isolated (one extreme) or co-dependent with a desperation for love and attention (the other extreme). The heart chakra is our most central and of the utmost importance. It gives us love, the most powerful healer of all, and loving ourselves is the foundation of good health and happiness. Remember the word *ahimsa?* The body parts that are affected are the chest, lungs, diaphragm, ribs, and heart. The sound is F.

Moving up from the root, we have the sacral chakra, orange in colour, and located just below our naval. This is about our sexuality and reproductive system and corresponds with the physical parts in this area of the body, so if we have issues with our hips, sacrum, womb, etc., then this is where the problem may lie on an energetic field. Its functions are to generate our sexual energies, creativity, new ideas, passions, and endurance. It gives physical force, vitality, and strength. The sound is the note D.

The solar plexus chakra is yellow and resides just below the rib cage. It gives us our sense of identity and personality. It promotes confidence, personal power, will, authority, humour, laughter, spontaneity, warmth, and an inner glow. Physically it connects with our ribs and digestive organs, and, if out of balance, we may become overpowering, overbearing, or strong willed. If unbalanced in the other direction, we may become weak, passive, and tired. The sound associated is E.

Above the heart we have the throat chakra, light blue in colour and connecting, quite obviously, with our throat. When in balance we communicate well, with clarity and confidence. It helps us connect to ourselves and the world around us. It also helps with our creativity including wanting to express ourselves vocally or on paper and, of course, with singing. If it is out of sync, we may clam up and become shy and introverted. Alternatively, we may talk too much; we are loud or scattered, or we command orders and are controlling. The body parts are the neck, throat, shoulders, tongue, mouth, and ears. The sound is G.

The chakra of the third eye is located at the centre of the forehead and is about connecting to our sixth sense, our inner knowing and wisdom—our vision, intuition, psychic abilities, concentration, self-knowledge, and insight. The colour is indigo, like a deep blue night sky. We attempt to quieten the mind to balance this chakra so as to achieve clarity and vision; otherwise, we maybe become close-minded and suffer delusions or even hallucinations. The parts of the body are the eyes, forehead, and, not too often talked about, pineal gland, which is a part of the body that fascinates me. The sound is A.

When our entire chakra system is out of balance, we can also become a little wobbly. If it becomes a regular imbalance, then this could manifest as a physical ailment or illness (remember stress) which is where spiritual healing and alternative therapies can be very beneficial. These might include acupuncture, reiki, Life Alignment, myofascial release, or rolfing, among others, because the practitioner is working with the out-of-balance energies, preferably before the imbalance becomes physical. 'Sound baths' are also very beneficial, as they provide the vibration associated with each chakra and work to heal the body parts in this area as well as the emotional trauma.

What we eat is also very relevant as food carries energy. For example, when we eat meat, we are not just ingesting the flesh of the animal but also the energy and fear that the beast experienced through its birth, life, and slaughter.

Think back to the tsunami of 2004. Apparently very few animals were found washed up on the shore after this tragedy; their sixth sense is still intact. They knew that a huge tidal wave was coming, the same as they know when they are about to be slaughtered. And, for the record, that fear, the related hormones, and the negative energy go into the flesh of the animal that you ingest. Yummy!

The chakra system also works on an emotional level and is just as vital.

Although all chakras have to be in balance for a full, correctly working system, our powerhouse is held within the solar plexus. This is our will centre, where we get to make decisions and learn to say no. How do you feel when you have to say 'no' to someone? Does it sometimes come out the wrong way, sounding like 'yes'?

> *Let's not forget that the little emotions are the great captains of our lives and we obey them without realising it.*

> —Vincent Van Gogh

There are many ways to balance our chakra system. Practising yoga is a great way, as various postures work with each individual vortex (chakra) and associated organs. In fact, the entire chakra system evolves from yoga. However, as mentioned previously, there are many other therapies and treatments to help bring them into alignment. Choosing to wear clothes or accessories that are the colour of a chakra can also be very empowering. But you have to be open and willing to make the change.

> *The purest and most thoughtful minds are those which love colour the most.*

> —John Ruskin, *The Stones of Venice*

A boss of mine once said that we have twenty-four hours in a day and this can be divided up as eight hours sleeping, eight hours working, and eight hours playing, as a general rule. I take this one step further and treat life a bit like a filing system. I said I'd come back to it, remember? It is helpful if we learn to put situations and emotions into little boxes, learning to compartmentalise and open them up as we need them. When the post comes through your door, there are three courses of action you can take. You can file it away when no action is necessary but you may need to refer to it later (think insurance policy documents, TV licence); you can bin/recycle it as it is superfluous to your needs (think junk mail); or you can take action (think bills and invitations). That piece of paper only needs to be touched once and not shuffled around on your kitchen table for weeks! Just like life!

Time for action! Grab a cup of tea. We are going to work through your wardrobe and look at what you've got.

I like to sort my clothes into colours so everything is 'filed' in the right order. For me, it's not quite *Sleeping with the Enemy*, but it gives me an idea as to what colour I need to wear that day, depending on how I feel. It is usually a subconscious decision. I have a friend (as I'm sure you do) who will only wear black. All the time. I realise some people wear this colour because they are in mourning or they think it makes them look slim, but it does nothing for their energetic, physical, or spiritual bodies. What do you associate with the colour black?

So now that you know a little about the chakra system, where do you feel *you* may be out of alignment the most? What are the colours in your wardrobe, and what would you like to work on to start with?

1. **Red** Root—Do you feel grounded, solid, balanced, connected to the earth? Do you look after your body well with diet, sleep, and exercise? Do you pay your bills on time? Is there room for improvement?

2. **Orange** sacral—Do you feel passionate and want to create new ideas? Are you getting enough sex and happy with the kind you are getting? Is it in balance? Are you content not to be sexually active? That's OK. Do you feel sexy? Would you like to?

3. **Yellow** Solar plexus—Can you make up your own mind, take decisions without procrastination? Do you say yes when deep inside you want to say no?

4. **Green** Heart—Are you open or closed, broken or bruised? Is it time to fill your heart with more love and share it with the outside? Are you afraid to open your heart?

5. **Blue** Throat—Do you feel restricted regarding your voice, your creativity? Are you timid, too quiet, frustrated perhaps? Are you the opposite: loud and over talkative? Are you being heard?

6. **Indigo** Third eye—Are you sometimes overpowering, overbearing, strong willed or, rather, the opposite, where you feel weak, passive, and tired? Are you intuitive? Do you follow your instincts?
7. **White** or **Purple** Crown—Do you feel disconnected, cynical, and materialistic or perhaps overly intellectual with an addiction to all things spiritual? Are you simply spaced out? Do you lack grounding?

Now go through and sort the clothes out that no longer serve you. Notice the colours that could help you on your path. Don't forget your underwear drawer!

If you have managed to recycle some clothes, did you include those that don't fit, still have the price tag on, that you will diet into, or you got for your graduation/daughter's christening/son's engagement, or whatever occasion? If you haven't worn them within the past six months (seasonal) then pass them on so they are recycled back into the world. They may have cost you a week's salary, but you are serving someone else now and giving them the opportunity to feel good about themselves. This is simply an exchange of energy.

Then you know what's next? We're going shopping! Decide what your body needs from the above chakra colour chart. Do not be tempted to buy something else; we are on a mission, and this is part of your healing process. The colour does not have to be on display to the world either. If you feel you are not grounded, you may like to invest in some red knickers, for example! You don't have to break the bank, either. It can be a small item to wear round your wrist as long as the colour is serving you. And remember, if you struggle in saying no, then yellow has got your name on it, lady!

Now we're done with the clothes, so what's next? Let's continue with your sleeping space by working through the rest of your dressing area and bedroom. Then move into the bathroom and the other bedrooms. Work your way around the house and declutter the items that no longer serve you. The colour is also relevant, by the way. Have you ever thought of inviting a Feng Shui expert to your house to assist in placing and removing objects? For romance, you may want to put pictures of loving couples in your bedroom or a pair of Chinese ducks, for example. Take out the TV and mirror. For wealth and prosperity, you may like to purchase a frog with a coin in its mouth or a money plant. These have to be placed in the correct position. Is your house sitting on a ley line or a position of negative energy? Is there water running underneath? Are you on a busy road?

Everything holds a memory, an energy, a thought of some sort, and the more you can remove from your home, the lighter you will feel and more detached you will become. You will start to feel free-er. This creates space for something more positive to move in and fill the void. I'm not saying these words lightly as I realise this is a mammoth task. Don't rush. Take a week or a month, but try and get it done before you move on to our next chapter. Start sorting out your household filing system.

If you really find this difficult, maybe you could reach out to a friend to help or your spouse or, even better still, one of your children. Treat it like a healthy cleanse of the past (which will always be there) and a celebration of the new congruent you that is emerging.

The final thing to do this week is a little bit of role play. I know this may sound weird, but if you are not good at saying no, today we are going to practice. And if you do struggle with this life skill I'm hoping you bought something yummy and yellow to wear; in fact, go and pop that on now to help empower you.

Now, take a moment to think about a couple of things that you have done because you didn't want to hurt the other person's feelings. Jot them down in your journal, and notice the sensations that come up in your body. Jot those down as well. Sit with the feelings. Allow the sensations to arise and just accept them. Then imagine that person asking you to do the task, and repeat the question out loud. Say no. Practice a few times saying no with more confidence and conviction and calmness. No need to be the fishwife that I once was. How is it feeling? Now stand in front of a full-length mirror and repeat the exercise. *Enjoy the sensation of the power you are taking back.*

Obviously don't go (yellow) bananas and start saying no to everything that comes your way because there are probably times you want to say yes! But when you really *don't* want to drive someone somewhere, fill in a work rota because someone was ill, or have another glass of wine that's being shoved your way, simply, firmly, and smilingly say no!

> *It's not who you are that holds you back, it's who you think you're not.*
>
> —Eleanor Roosevelt

Things to-do list:

1. Wardrobe purge—'File' your clothes into colours, and pull out and recycle those that no longer serve you.
2. Decide on the chakra you wish to work on the most and go shopping!
3. Put on something yellow and let's role-play saying no!
4. Declutter the house—the more space you create, the more room you make for something positive and powerful and fun to fill it. Be ruthless!
5. Consider contacting a Feng Shui expert to lighten up the energy in your living space.
6. Write down what would be your biggest deathbed regret. Write it down in big, bold letters.

In the next chapter, we will look at forgiveness and how this is key to happiness and peace within. Remember you are only part way through your life, and this is the end of one chapter as we turn the pages to another!

Chapter 5

MY LIFE SEEMS OVER

Put your future in good hands – your own.

—Ralph Waldo Emerson

I say to you today, my friends, that in spite of the difficulties and frustrations of the moment, I still have a dream.

—Martin Luther King, Jr

LET'S TAKE A RECAP OF what we have done so far. In chapter 1 you learned that anything goes here: crying, screaming, feeling miserable, etc. All is welcome and you are in a safe place. Chapter 2 was about feelings and physical reactions, and we talked about pebbles. Bear in mind, not every pebble wants to be picked up and chucked back into a cold lake. They've already done the work to get out of the water and stay on dry land! In chapter 3, you glanced back at some favourite activities and ways to relax, and you also considered ways to put your life skills into service. Then in chapter 4, we had a go at reclaiming power by saying *no* to things that didn't serve you.

So tonight, Josephine, in chapter 5, we are going to look at forgiveness and gratitude. These are so powerful for giving us back our freedom. Let me explain.

You are what your deep, driving desire is. Remember those words! I have been married now for over twenty-four years, my first and only marriage, yet I have nearly divorced (which included trips to the solicitor) more times than Elizabeth Taylor. When it was hubby's turn to divorce me, he actually wanted to do a selfie (divorce not photo), so we filled in the forms online and posted them. Overnight he had a change of heart, so he got up early and waited for the postman to collect the mail. Having explained his turn-around to Postman Pat, he was very fortunate (or not) to be given back the divorce papers that he had meticulously filled in. At that time, I saw myself as the demon and went along with what had been written; I even helped type it up! We have had a lot of tit for tat in our marriage, and I assume that this is normal. (Although I know that to assume can make an ASS out of U and ME!) In fact, I see this in most relationships because this is what life is all about, and we are here to grow and learn. *The only way we can learn about ourselves is in relationship.* It took me a long time to come to terms with that fact, and I didn't like it. But once I was made aware of it, with reluctance, I accepted it and it has served me well. *All* the opportunities that come my way I am grateful for, even the shitty ones, because it is in those ones that I can develop the most as a human being. That is why, in my humble opinion, we are roaming this planet.

I don't know if it is an egotistical kind of thing or just a get-out clause, but I, in my heart of hearts, feel that we have many attempts at being human. It is a yogic philosophy as well and part of many other belief systems. Regardless, I do believe in re-incarnation, and it is because of this belief that I have absolutely no fear of death (I think!) I'm not sure if I will enjoy the physical transition, but I'm pretty sure the spiritual one will be one heck of a ride. I am also re-assured because I sense my Mum and Dad will have dinner ready for when I get there—or whatever the equivalent is in heaven!

People meditate to find peace, happiness, enlightenment, and all good things, and without a doubt there is room for meditation in my life. At times, this turns into *mediation* instead as the 't' is often accidentally dropped. In fact, my friend Sally said she would be out of touch for two weeks as she was on a mediation course. I was quite envious, and when we met for lunch I asked what kind of meditating she did. Was it silent, Vipassana, walking? *Medi-ation,* she said. No 't'! She now uses that precious skill in running her business and managing staff, but also, she said, in private relationships.

So let's stick the t back in for a moment and imagine you were a monk/ess and had been sitting in the hills for the past ten years, meditating, finding the meaning of life. Then you found all the answers, so you came back down town to have a cup of tea or maybe a hot chocolate (dairy free). You've been so blissed out for the past ten years that when you walk into the coffee shop, you are stunned that it is hot, busy, noisy, and there's nowhere to sit. Someone bumps into you, spilling hot liquid on your bare foot. Whatever occurs is a wake-up call because you are back to mixing with people. You have to deal with the emotions that stir up inside you.

I'm not dissing meditation (or mediation) in any form here. I'm trying to illustrate that it is people who *make us feel,* and although this is a challenge, this is also a fantastic thing. We need people in order to experience the joys of love/pain, anger/laughter, frustration/calmness, good/bad, day/night, hot/cold, black and white. All these opposites allow us to express who we are and learn from experiences. Do we push the person out the way when they accidentally spill their tea on our foot, or do we forgive them, from the heart? Do we tolerate the noise around us with a relaxed smile on our face, or do we grit our teeth and whinge about it to the waitress or to ourselves?

Being in relationship allows us to find the man behind the mirror, inside the mirror, underneath that magnifying glass. The relationship does not have to be with your spouse either. The hot tea incident was with a stranger, but it still aroused emotion. By the way, we will come back to meditation in chapter 9 because there certainly is a place for it (in my mind!) Because of this mutual growth, being in a partnership, marriage, or long-term relationship is an absolute gift, even if we are not happy.

Warning: If your partner is abusive, either physically or emotionally, I urge you to get out. And if that is easier said than done, you must seek help. Do not, under any circumstances, allow another person to bully you, especially a lover or a spouse, whether mentally, verbally, or physically. *Under any circumstances.*

In chapter 4 I mentioned I was a party animal, and, even at my age, I still like to party. But I do so on the edge now. By that, I mean I no longer lose myself in all the fun a party can provide. My parties are very different now but just as much fun, if not more so. When I was younger, like most,

I thoroughly enjoyed a good time, but I came to realise I was relying on *things* to provide the good time for me, such as alcohol, food, wine, music, smoking, even friends. Don't get me wrong, some of this stuff is great, but I have found I enjoy life with more awareness since I have knocked some of them on the head (not literally of course!) Certain things we need, for sure, as I said previously, because people have to bounce off each other. We see the faults that we all possess by looking into the eyes of the other. Michael Jackson sang about this. I was told once that he used to run many of his lyrics by Deepak Chopra for assurance and advice.

> *Whatever relationships you have attracted in your life at this moment, are precisely the ones you need in your life at this moment. There is a hidden meaning behind all events, and this hidden meaning is serving your own evolution.*

> —Deepak Chopra

And this, from Michael Jackson's 'Man in the Mirror'

I've been a victim of a selfish kind of love
It's time that I realise
That there are some with no home, not a nickel
to loan
Could it be really me, pretending that they're
not alone?

Listen to the song and perhaps the above verse will have more meaning for you as Michael sings about starting with the man in the mirror. Very poignant. We look in the mirror to make sure we are clean, tidy, and presentable to the outside world. But do we notice what lies beneath? Hardly. We walk around wearing a mask most of the time, trying to please people and trying to be happy. And, in trying to be happy for ourselves, we end up trying to please people. It's a bit of a circle.

When my husband and I were going through one of our divorce conversations, we thought we'd take the dogs out for a walk. 'Coo-ie!' I heard in the distance. I looked up and saw Melinda, my neighbour. We had both been to a recent puppy party, and she was walking her beautiful pup as well. Other than that, I'd never said more than one polite sentence to her in probably ten years. 'May I join you?' she asked. 'Yes,' I said. (I was obviously not wearing yellow.) It was not a very enjoyable walk because hubby and I were at loggerheads, but we were trying to be polite to her when really we should have said no. We wanted to be liked.

Being in a long-term commitment allows us to grow if we let it, but we need to be open to this. Everything we see in that person, the good and the bad, is the same that we have in our own being. Does that make sense? So when you don't like the fact that hubby doesn't load the dishwasher the right way, and it *annoys* you, perhaps you get frustrated. But what about when you leave a sticky spoon in the sugar bowl, and that annoys him? Obviously, these are very basic examples, but try to understand the science behind it, like an equation. Sorry, that's maths not science. Never mind.

The point is that we are *constantly* being triggered by situations, and how we react to them is the key to our happiness. This is the key to our strength, our growth. But just understanding these words is not the answer. We need to experience them.

My husband and I muddle along quite well now. We have gone through so many rollercoaster challenges in our marriage, but now we are both on the same page and so much stronger because of our experiences. We hung in there! But the marriage is nothing like it used to be—pre-children. Having children definitely played a huge part in the dents in our relationship. Although I still loved my husband, I kind of pushed him aside and fell in love with my children instead. Basic really. Like the lioness or, heaven forbid, that black widow. I think the only animal that works differently is the penguin. If you haven't seen *March of the Penguins,* I urge you to grab a copy this weekend. Delightful documentary and I won't spoil it for you.

In any case, when we start filling the nest with children, our role changes from lover to mother. We made ourselves pretty and gorgeous and attracted our mate with our pheromones, then managed to pro-create and have a baby, so hubby has served his purpose. Although there are lots of jobs round the house to do, dear. We then start fluffing our nest and concentrate on bringing up our offspring. This is a huge task because we still have a husband to please, and life becomes very busy and difficult. The breasts are to feed the babies not to be fondled at 2.00 a.m. when you would rather have a back rub (and leave it at that). We start wearing two hats, and eventually the thread wears thin. Cracks appear in the relationship, but they can be filled and the foundation of your nest can become stronger—if you are open to these words and prepared to work at it. Of course, both people are involved in this change because this is a relationship. No one person is to be blamed. Remember the ripple effect of the pebble in the lake? Everything is connected, and, by taking care of yourself, it will have an effect on everyone and everything around you. Therefore, you have to stay strong in your own shoes here. Think of the colours you are wearing.

Returning to marriage after kids, we become more focussed on bringing up our children. Natural, normal. At this stage of our lives, we don't think too far ahead because we think our children are ours forever. Big mistake! They are not ours. We are caretakers of them to teach them the right things to do in the world, so they can go off and live their lives with solid foundations. Remember how we teach the man to fish? It is very easy for some of us to live our lives *for* our children rather than alongside them.

My hubby and I love living in the English countryside and still have a few animals left though several have moved to animal heaven. We recently acquired more pre-loved, second-hand cats. When I was younger, I wanted to marry a farmer, preferably in Canada; I thought it would be wonderful working outdoors with the animals. I know now that times have changed, so thank goodness that never happened! Farmers have laws unto themselves. They multiply everything as much as they can and cut down trees and woodland in the name of agriculture. Then they stick either more animals or a building on top to make money.

On one of my long country walks, I noticed a farmer raping the fields with diggers and big heavy machinery and casually asked what the purpose was but was promptly told to mind my own business, as I did not need to 'police the area'. But this is where they are wrong. 'The trees cannot speak for themselves,' I said. They need to be protected. When we die, we do not take the fields with us, or the trees or the land. Nothing, in fact, not even the overcoat skin we have worn for ninety years. We are *caretakers* and that is something we must remember, whether it is for the land, the animals, or our children. But some people do not understand this, and this is where the pain can arise. We become too attached. The more we attach ourselves to something, the harder it is to let go. We can still love and care for the people, items, possessions, but we must learn to let them go without being emotional. This is not the same as indifference. Feelings are still involved here, but we do not lose control. By all means, feel passion, but do not be over-passionate, experience emotions but don't become over-emotional.

When we are in control of our emotions, we think more clearly. When we experience our emotions, good or bad, we are living a healthy life; we just need to learn to accept the emotions that arise in us. It is important for us to value the people and the items that are bestowed on us throughout life, but it is essential to know that we can exist contentedly without them. This all stems from how we perceive and react to situations. Remember that monk again.

We all carry a little bit of Hitler in us (check out Mother Theresa), but even the genuine caretakers that spend their life devoted to helping others, have a shadow side. But by recognising this shadow self, this dark side that is part of the human condition, we can learn to work with it. Being *grateful* for the good feelings *and* the bad feelings is a start to finding both spiritual and physical abundance, as hard as that may be to comprehend.

I have undertaken many courses in my life in an effort to make myself a better person and discover why we are here, where are we from, and where are we going. I do feel that I am here not just to learn but also to illustrate to others, which is the purpose behind this book. In my seeking, I have discovered that it is all right to feel good and it is also just as OK to feel bad, though obviously not quite as nice an experience. The point I am trying to make is that *we are feeling*. We are being human and we are therefore *living* our life. Sometimes we get stuck, though, and start merely enduring our life. That's when we miss the point. Never forget that you are a human *being*.

Take yourself back to when your children were young and you were at the playground with them, sitting at the opposite end of the see-saw. To make our little people feel comfortable and safe, we would keep our legs on the ground while theirs would dangle, remember? Then, very slowly, we would push off with our feet so we would go a little higher and they would go lower—up and down. This is life. When we are up, everything is fab-a-doodle-dandy. We look around and see the wonders of the world from our dizzying heights. But we know we have to come down. And we do, sometimes with a bang. When we are down, we look up to see our Little Tommy giggling over his ride. Although you can see he is having fun, and you are too, it's not quite as good as being up in the air. However, your turn will come. Ultimately you try to get a balance of going up and down. This is how life 'should' be (I don't like the word 'should').

But before you get to go up or down, you have to reach the middle bit, where Little Tommy is at the same level as you. Now if you firmly set in your mind that this is the place we always get back to, it will become easier to release the stuff that you are not happy with in your life. When you are up, and everything is full of sunshine, just remember that these feelings are not sustainable or permanent and you will have to come down. But that's fine. Then comes the hard bit. When you are down, remember that it doesn't rain every day, but try to *understand* those sensations whilst you are there, knowing that you will be back up in due course. See if you can enjoy feeling miserable! When you get really good at this, you may find you don't need the ups or the downs. You have an awareness that whatever life throws at you is part of the human condition, and how you react to it is the key. This is why I no longer need to go to wild parties.

When I found out there were three people in our marriage, I was not high up on my see-saw. In fact, I dug a hole and went below ground. I had lost my father; I had an awareness that my children would ultimately leave the nest as they were becoming increasingly independent; and then I realised that my husband did not 'belong' to me. It's not necessary to give you the exciting details, but I felt rejected, lonely, unhappy, and miserable. There was nothing to do other than confront my husband about the third party, and one of our divorce attempts ensued.

I came home one night after living separately from my husband, albeit at opposite ends of the same house, and there was a handwritten letter on my pillow. Initially I wanted to bin it as I thought it would be full of more shit. It was a love letter, from him. To me. I still disliked him intensely (I don't like to use the word hate) but something inside me stirred. It was a glimmer of opportunity. I had been gifted with the opportunity to forgive.

Dr Wayne Dyer tells of his story. When he was a child, his father walked out on his mother and five children. As an adult, Wayne searched tirelessly for his father, burdened with anger, resentment, and bitterness. One day he discovered that his father was, in fact, dead. Not content, he continued to search for the graveyard where his father was buried. He eventually found it and looked for the headstone. When he arrived at the foot of the grave, he spent a long time shouting out his anger, hurt, and bitterness. He then started to walk away. But before he left, he paused, turned round, walked back to the plot, and said quietly, 'Dad, I forgive you'. At that moment, the weight that had borne down on Wayne's shoulders, the clouds that had shadowed his every move, dissipated. It was then that he could return home and write his best-seller *Your Erroneous Zones*, which sold over thirty-five million copies.

By taking away all the anger and hatred that stands in our way, we can replace it with love. This is the most healing and empowering thing that we can do. With your body filled with love, so many things in your life will change. We all need love, but we don't need revenge. Who was it that said, *forgive them, Father, for they know not what they do*. In learning to forgive, start with yourself.

In bringing up your children, you must be aware that you have done your bit in keeping the human race alive. That is a huge contribution to society. And you only buy free range eggs, don't you? So let your grown children roam free.

Of course, there are times you may feel overcome with grief at the emptiness of your nest, and you may struggle with guilt for all the good things that you still have in your life. This is absolutely normal, a human feeling. But now is *your* time. Like this book, we live our lives in chapters, and you have the opportunity to experience a new one.

> *Forgiveness is the most powerful thing you can do for yourself on the spiritual path. If you can't learn to forgive, you can forget about getting to higher levels of awareness.*
>
> —Dr Wayne Dyer

Things to-do list:

1. List the people that have hurt you and how.
2. Write down the lessons available to you from these life experiences.
3. Write a letter of forgiveness to these individuals, post it, burn it, or bury it.
4. Think about which relationships bring joy to your life and why. Which don't and why?
5. Write down the times you have done something you didn't want to just so that you would be liked.

In the next chapter, we will look at our boundaries as well as the importance of associating with like-minded and positive people to help us grow and find our true purpose.

Chapter 6

TIRED OF LYING TO A STRANGER: RECOVER, RECLAIM, AND MANAGE YOUR PERSONAL POWER

There are only two ways to live your life. One is as though nothing is a miracle. The other is as though everything is a miracle.

—Albert Einstein.

Boundaries are very important and sometimes difficult to ascertain. When we moved from our town house to the country, one of our new neighbours very politely welcomed us to the area and, in the same conversation, explained that a part of the land we had purchased belonged to them. Fortunately, the deeds were fresh in my mind, so I could 'put them right' straight away, but of course, it didn't leave a good impression although we have managed to co-exist for sixteen years without too much grief.

As my property portfolio started to grow and my business expanded, I ventured into development. I purchased a quirky holiday home and, after a couple of years, decided to convert this into five apartments. I was sandwiched between two gentlemen whom I discovered didn't like women, or perhaps they just didn't like me. The one on the right owned the private road where my property was located, and, although I had full access, he didn't want me to use it to build unless he received a third of the uplift (profit). Of course, I refused, so he blocked the entrance, preventing my trucks from getting through. It took over three years and in excess of £100,000 for me to defend my case, hiring solicitors and barristers and going to the High Court in London. Even though I knew I was right both legally and morally, there were times that I actually doubted it. This was because of my neighbour's sheer bloody mindedness, coupled with the fact that legal people compare court to a game of poker. Not very re-assuring, especially as they weren't holding the dice.

Fortunately for me (and the bank), I won, but this cost my neighbour not just his pride but in excess of £200,000 and a fallout with virtually all the people in the neighbourhood because he had installed unsightly shipping containers on the road to cause more complications.

If we don't put our foot down, then we get trodden on, and it takes a great deal of energy and effort to stand up to bullies. We find these sort of people through all walks of life, and many of them hide behind a uniform. It is scary how a simple uniform can instil fear in people, and I personally think the world is being controlled to deliberately and falsely increase fear. Think of how we are treated now when we go on holiday. Take off your shoes, stand over there, empty your liquids, stand inside this radiation machine. And how do we react? We go along with it. We even allow people to drag us, or fellow passengers, from a paid-for flight without batting an eyelid until after the event. 'Sheeple' is an understatement.

> *The only thing necessary for the triumph of evil is for good men to do nothing.*

> —Edmund Burke

My latest argument is the dreaded parking ticket at a train station. I parked without causing any obstruction or inconvenience on black tarmac that was unmarked, but I did not follow instructions and park within white lines. There were no lines where I parked, just a huge, vacant space. Plus, this car park is free! But a uniform decided to stick a parking ticket (actually an invoice) on my windscreen. I refused to pay, and it has escalated (for misbehaving) to £206 and still counting.

I continue to dispute this, and I'll let you know the outcome when we get there ... I got there. They backed down!

Some bullies don't need to wear a uniform to control us. We bump into them throughout life's torn rug, and some of us end up in relationship with them. If this is you, the positive side is that you have a great opportunity to grow; however, it could be a painful process.

In the transition to becoming an empty nester, we encounter many new people in our new life. We may feel raw and vulnerable as we start to make friends because it may have been a while since we opened up to a new face. We may throw ourselves into experiences that aren't right for us, or we may decide to avoid checking out our new best buddies.

In one school of psychotherapy, people can be categorised into five different character types, and it is important to know that other people can use your energy in their favour; it can be fertile ground for abuse to happen. Understanding certain traits in people can be a start in getting your power back, even if you didn't know you gave it away! Have a look at these:

Schizoid

This personality tends to blame others for their issues due to trauma they suffered either *in utero*, during birth, or in the early days afterwards. Their body shape would tend to be tall, thin, and elongated because, energetically, their soul is stretching up and trying to return to source, often attempting to leave the body. They are uncoordinated, with left and right imbalances and weak, thin wrists, ankles, calves, and joints because they are not very grounded. Their hands and feet are cold, and their head may often be held to one side with a vague look in their eyes. They may find it difficult to connect to people as they possess an inner fear due to their early trauma. They are very wilful in personality and do not like to live in the here and now, so they are very ungrounded and hyperactive. You may be familiar with the phrase *they are besides themselves*, which implies their soul has left the body and is alongside it. They tend to be very spiritual and creative people who have experienced many lifetimes. In relationship, in the back of their mind, they always want to reject you before you reject them. They talk in absolutes and in a depersonalised manner.

Oral

The oral personality fears abandonment because they have suffered the loss of their mother during the early stages of childhood, either physically or emotionally. To compensate this painful feeling, the child will become independent too early, which may manifest by talking and walking prematurely. They learn to be frightened of asking for their needs in case what they want is not given. As the personality develops, they feel empty—hollow—and avoid being alone. Sexuality is used to find connection and closeness. Physically this character has an undeveloped body with long, thin, smooth, weak muscles. They do not look like a mature adult and have a sunken, cold, depressed chest with shallow breathing. They are depleted of energy, and you may feel their eyes sucking your energy when you look into them. They evoke the mothering instinct in you and act with passivity, neediness, and dependency. They communicate through constant questioning.

Psychopathic

This character should come with a warning sign stamped on their forehead. They have experienced a covertly seductive parent of the opposite sex in their childhood and, sadly, found it difficult to get support from the other parent of the same sex. They therefore side with the other one in a manipulative manner because they could not get what they wanted and felt betrayed. This experience evolves into trying to control others with demands to be supported and encouraged. They have a tremendous drive for power and to dominate and manipulate others by bullying or using seduction. They tend to have many sexual fantasies with feelings of superiority and contempt, which hides their inferiority complex. They always want to win and find it difficult to surrender.

Physically, the upper body is large, with a lack of energetic flow to the lower half, and the pelvis is undercharged, cold, and tightly held. The chest is top heavy and inflated. They have cold, weak legs, and they are of a hyperactive nature, followed by wanting to collapse. There is severe tension in the shoulders, base of skull, and eyes, and they are not grounded. They are torn between their dependency on people (with their need to control), and they are terrified of becoming the victim, which they would find humiliating. They try to make others need them, and they may at times go into a rage. Internally, they live a life of fantasy with heroic adventures of honour, truth, and honesty and would love to bring this into their real life.

Masochistic

This personality had a mother who gave love conditionally and in a dominating and sacrificing manner, perhaps to the extent of controlling the child's eating and toilet-ing habits. The child was made to feel guilty if he started to assert a sense of freedom or individuality and was crushed in these attempts, so he felt trapped, defeated, and humiliated. He would hold on to any feelings of creativity in an attempt to compensate, and this would lead to anger and hatred. Although this character wants to be independent, when interacting with others he is overly polite but also tends to whine in disgust in an effort to manipulate others. He then gets angrier from people's reactions and is caught up in a circle. On the outside it looks like he is gentle and submissive, but he is not and never will be. The blocked feelings of spite, negativity, hostility, superiority, and fear may explode into a violent rage. He may have a strong interest in porn, and the female masochistic character may not experience orgasms with the belief that her sexuality is unclean. Generally this is a negative person.

Physically the body is heavy and compacted, with overdeveloped muscles and a shortening of the neck and waist. There is strong tension in the neck; jaw; throat; and pelvis, which is tucked under, whilst the head thrusts forward. They hold back feelings and they love to whinge. They can be provocative, so as to create an excuse to explode; however, they are unaware they are provoking and think that they are acting in a pleasing manner. Generally, the masochistic types are aggressive and boiling inside.

Rigid

The child with a rigid character structure suffered rejection by the parent of the opposite sex, which they took to be a betrayal of love. According to a child with a rigid disposition, erotic pleasure, sexuality, and love are all the same. To compensate the child learns to control all the feelings of pain and rage, as well as the good feelings, holding them back. To release these feelings, she eventually has to surrender, which is a scary scenario, so, instead, she becomes manipulative to get what she wants. A rigid character type holds back feelings so as not to look foolish. She is worldly, ambitious, and competitively aggressive, holding the belief that she is superior and knows everything, but inside there is a fear of betrayal. She does not want to feel vulnerable and is very afraid of being hurt.

Physically, the head is held high and the spine stands straight with pride. There is a high degree of outer control and a strong identification of physical reality, and this strong ego is used as an excuse to avoid letting go. She does not go with the flow. Sex for this type is performed with contempt and not love. By holding back their feelings, they create more pride within themselves, demanding love and sexual intimacy from others. They do not remain committed, so a circle is created whereby they choose sex over love to avoid any chance of getting hurt.

Physically the body is harmoniously proportioned, and highly energised and integrated. The pelvis is tipped back and energetically cold. They are hyperactive and live by the mind and the will. With a rigid back and hyperactive personality, they evoke competition and use the language of seduction.

* * * * *

Although everybody carries an element of all these character structures, the ones that will tend to give you the most grief are the psychopaths, so often dramatised in the movies. While exciting to watch, it's best to avoid this relationship if you can spot them coming!

In our search for happiness and meaning, we often join different clubs, groups, associations or become part of a religion to feel connected to others. People are supposed to be in community, and the breakdown of the traditional, vital, and healthy family nucleus has opened up many opportunities for us to get involved in different societies. People need people and I think this is a good thing, depending on the association you are drawn to.

Many years ago, I joined an organisation in an attempt to become a trained spiritual healer. I had illusions of being the next Jesus Christ, where I would set out to heal the world. I'm sure there comes a time in many people's life when we want to heal the word. Although I learned a great deal from their syllabus, I also learned a great deal that wasn't on it.

I have always been drawn to helping people. In my twenties I volunteered as a Samaritan, where I met a fellow volunteer who was a spiritual healer. He was very inspirational and on the same wavelength as me. He encouraged me to follow this path, and I have since trained in many therapies; crystal healing, angelic realms, hypnotherapy, tarot reading, reiki, and ultimately I was lead to *Healing Hands*. I loved this group; they were the family I had always searched for, and, within the first week, I felt that cliché: I was home. I think that's what a lot of us say these days when we feel we have connected with a group of like-minded beings. Now I realise that this isn't quite the case.

During the second year of the course, I came into my own. We were studying the second chakra, and you may recall that this is to do with creativity and sexuality. There was a woman in my cohort who began to attach herself to me. She liked me and thought I was funny, which made me feel good about myself. I wish I'd seen the warning signs, but in those days, I didn't know what they were.

She was often telling us that she had not had sex for some time and was quite flirtatious. I kept suggesting interested parties for her to pursue. Several of us shared the same hotel and would have pyjama parties as we chatted late into the night. In the beginning I didn't realise I was attracted to her. She was very boyish and would never wear a bra, so you could see her small breasts and brown nipples through her crisp white shirt—no this is not turning into a Jackie Collins novel. I just want you to get the picture. She was a seductress.

The more we hung out together, the closer we got. She would persist in giving me reflexology and massage treatments, and when we had to return home after a week of coursework, she'd get up early to see me off, thrusting a CD into my hands that she had compiled the night before. All the songs were perfect.

One night, as a pyjama party came to a close, her flirting went one step further and she pounced on me. That night was one I will certainly not forget. I took this new experience in my stride as she raised my status to pedestal level. Gifts galore and compliments that my husband had never used. Not on me anyway. Once again I was hooked. Sex, lust, and carnal pleasure had risen its ugly head.

He is lost who is possessed by carnal desire.

—Mahatma Gandhi

Yes, I did tell my husband. I had taken him to the pub for his birthday and bestowed the knowledge as a gift. I thought he'd be thrilled. I could imagine a ménage à trois every so often. I thought this may be a way to solve my problem, by bringing them both together so I could have my cake and eat it. Big mistake. 'Just don't go falling in love,' he said. I thought he was joking. The thought had never crossed my mind as I noticed a tear in the corner of his eye.

But eventually I did. I fell in what I thought was love, and only years later did I learn the difference between being *in love* and loving someone. Part of me will always be grateful to this Terrible Tomboy for the period of my life we shared intimately, even though it was incredibly painful and destructive. For many. You see, she was a psychopath by nature, the one that sucks the energy out of you for their own needs and progression. She was constantly saying how I was good for her, but I never read those signs. When she dropped me from that exceedingly high pedestal, I shattered into tiny pieces once again, but on this occasion it seemed worse because she was a woman. I thought it was only men that were bastards.

Having allowed her into my world, I gave her power to infiltrate my energy field, and, although I could sense it was happening, I was powerless to resist because *I allowed her to make me feel good about myself.* The aftermath and carnage was indescribable. I had risked my marriage and family, rocked my entire foundation, and allowed someone to get right inside my heart with a dagger and twist it, several times. It took me a very long time to get over this ordeal; at times, I even had suicidal thoughts to relieve myself from the pain. I had become obsessed.

I no longer blame her, and it has been many years since I flinched at her name or when I hear one of the songs she presented to me. Again, I was provided with a fabulous opportunity to learn more about myself. But I was totally devastated, and there were many occasions when I did not want to remain on this planet.

All this became public information in the bubble that was our healing school. People love to get involved with gossip and to chuck advice left, right, and centre. However, the scariest part for me was the lack of support provided by the school.

As part of the course, we had to sign up for regular weekly therapy with counsellors who had already completed the training and continued to a more advanced level of training, within the organisation. They were very expensive sessions, and this was part of the condition of being a student. I had two practitioners, as I wanted to become a great healer, and I would discuss, in detail, my predicament with them: about my husband, my children, my life, and this intruder who had made a habit of entering into established relationships. I later discovered I was not the first triangle she had created.

My counsellors were utterly useless. From the outset, I had shared my experience with them, *but not once* was I discouraged from continuing nor was any consideration given to my husband or my three young children. My family unit. Or me.

As the end was dawning, they encouraged us both to share *our process* to the entire group (over forty students plus teachers), which I felt was disempowering, belittling, and entirely unhelpful. Some students came up to me, delighting in my vulnerability, and in the end, I realised the only way I could escape was to leave, which I did. As I had done thirty years earlier when I ran away from home, after breakfast whilst everybody was making their way to their next class, I sneaked out the door on a pre-booked flight. It was my birthday, and I spent it entirely alone at an airport hotel, which turned out to be my strength; a transition from one chapter of my life to the next. There was only *one* person who encouraged me to walk away from this ordeal, including family and friends. Thank you Jo! Everyone else told me to see it through because of the three years and extortionate fees I had invested. And, I wanted to be a healer.

On a sad note about this school of healing, I have never come across *anyone* who offers this healing service after having completed the work. On a very serious note, three people, two of whom I had become quite close to, committed suicide not long after. Very scary stuff. I am not saying the school is responsible, but some cults do attract a certain sort of person but are unable to support them in the process when things get tricky. I was not contacted once by a staff member when I left, and I even followed up my departure with a letter. For all they know, I could have been another statistic. The teachers were simply students who had done a couple more years at the institute than I had. No other formal training was required.

Through my trials and tribulations, I have learned that the only person to make me feel good about myself is me. And that's a crucial lesson. I have learned to set my boundaries, whether this is with neighbours, tenants, family, friends, or organisations.

In giving ourselves permission to be happy, it is important to surround ourselves with positive people, not those that suck us dry for their own needs, the psychopathic Draculas in this world. Can you think of any in your life? This may, surprisingly, include your best friend or your parents, and you may not even be aware that they are taking your energy. Don't feel guilty about it. A fact is a fact. There are certainly times when children leave home and we end up parenting our parents. Sometimes we are the filling in the sandwich and have to look after both sides.

In learning to protect ourselves, we do not have to stop seeing them. On the contrary we can grow from this awareness (because this is all about relationship, remember). Instead we moderate the time we spend with them and choose the place carefully. This doesn't mean you have to stop hanging out with the girl you grew up with if you have worked out that she is bad news. It means you need to be aware of the problem and be less giving of yourself. It's the same as saying no. Pace yourself. Don't always be around and don't always let these people suck your energy because they will and they will bring you down. One way to protect yourself is to imagine yourself in a huge golden bubble of light, shaped like an egg. This way they will not be able to penetrate your energy field, which is what they have been doing.

In interaction with our friends we often call on our ego, which creates a role for us. But remember *ahimsa;* trust yourself and your inner feelings. Be kind to yourself with non-violence. Don't do things if you don't want to. Listen to your body. When you are in good relationship with your emotions, you can share with others. Look towards yourself. We are sensitive beings, but it is important to be centred within ourselves.

A person who fights with herself also fights with the world and vice versa. It is like the energy of a hedgehog; when they are in fear, they turn into a ball and spikes appear. Nobody can blame you for protecting yourself, and you won't be hurt if you don't want to be. But it is necessary that you do not want someone to hurt you and are aware of it. Be careful what you think and what you wish for because it tends to be accomplished. If you think the world is a hostile place, then it will be. Therefore, fill your life with positive, loving, and giving souls.

Who in your life do you find inspirational? What about the famous people you've heard of—the Ghandis and John Lennons? How do they inspire you? Is this because you want to be like them or you are encouraged by their creativity, success, beauty, strength? In looking for these qualities, be sure to know that these are beneath the skin. You are not impressed because of how they look on the outside; it is how they look and behave on the inside that counts.

So in closing this chapter, remember that it is important to love yourself because you deserve the best (*ahimsa*).

> *Cherish your solitude. Take trains by yourself to places you have never been. Sleep out alone under the stars. Learn how to drive a stick shift. Go so far away that you stop being afraid of not coming back. Say no when you don't want to do something. Say yes if your instincts are strong, even if everyone around you disagrees. Decide whether you want to be liked or admired. Decide if fitting in is more important than finding out what you're doing here. Believe in kissing.*
>
> —Eve Ensler

Things to-do list:

1. List the people in your life who tend to suck your energy and describe how they do so.
2. Think up ways to prevent this and set your boundaries.
3. List the people you love being with and reasons why.
4. List people who inspire you.
5. List the qualities you see in yourself that these inspirational people have.

In the next chapter we take a look at how we can become more connected with ourselves through self-care, mantra, and music.

Chapter 7

WHAT THE HECK DO I DO NOW - LEARNING TO FULLY CARE FOR YOURSELF AGAIN

Never be bullied into silence. Never allow yourself to be made a victim. Accept no one's definition of your life; define yourself.

—Harvey Fierstein

VIRABHADRASANA IS THE SANSKRIT NAME for warrior pose in yoga; there are I, II and III of them, and when we practice in class, I don't see men fighting on the battlefield; I see strong, independent women (and men) holding their own, just in that moment of time. Whatever goes on outside our yoga practice is irrelevant. These women are strong, courageous, determined, and standing in their own skin, even if it is for only ninety minutes per week. My classes are not to make people perform wonderful bendy positions just to look great, but to help empower the individual so they can come into their own.

I mentioned before that my mother was a warrior even though she left one controlling situation for another. She courageously left home at twenty-one to move south from Liverpool to reconnect with my father, whom she had met on a holiday camp a couple of years before. She found a job in a children's home in Rustington. She returned there once my father died, and I always felt it was in the hope that she would catch a memory, a glimpse of him across a crowded street or perhaps in Woolworths, where he used to pinch a sweet from the Pick 'n' Mix. I remember mimicking him once, and he scolded me! I never understood why.

Mum would tell us horror stories of her life as a child. Her mother didn't have a proper kitchen, and a leaking corrugated sheet of metal served as the roof of a tiny room, with rainwater pouring in at times. Her father was a bully. He would return from a trip on the merchant seas, often bringing back exotic animals. Mum would excite us with tales of crocodiles in the bath tub and a monkey named Jacko who used to sit on the hanging wooden clothes dryer and pee on the Liverpool Insurance man's hat, when he came to collect money each Wednesday at teatime. She would tell us how she loved to dress up her little brothers and charge a shilling to perform shows for the neighbourhood kids. These were interlaced with sad stories about her dad telling her and her siblings to be in bed when he got back from the pub. That's when he put bruises all over my grandmother's face because she hadn't kept the house clean enough. My mum was frightened of going home at times in case her mother had carried out her threat of putting her head in the gas oven.

So when my dear mother escaped to Sussex, she had met her Prince Charming, and they were going to live happily ever after. My mother stood her ground, but she didn't have a lot of it to stand on. Dad was a very good, honourable, and honest man; he took care of his family the only way he knew how, but this was with a high degree of strictness. He had his own very tough upbringing in utter poverty as well. Because of his authoritarian values, I guess that's why I legged it at seventeen, but my mother couldn't.

When my father died, the whole family were in shock. How could someone so strong, determined, wise, and loving disappear? We just didn't get it. All that life experience, knowledge, love, and physical presence just gone, in a puff of smoke.

My mother's empty nest was now totally bare. We tried to fill it with love and visits and grandchildren and whatever else we could, but her heart had been snapped in two. This was also especially hard for us three kids as we felt we had lost part of our mother as well, even though we were all grown up, physically, at least. I certainly felt this way. There was always a distance in my mother's expression and words, as much as she tried to hide it. People that didn't know my parents too well didn't get it because my parents bickered and argued constantly. Even whilst my father was suffering with cancer, Mum would make comments about how she may be the first to go if she got run over by a bus. It was weird and quite remarkable, this co-dependent relationship they had. She was the nagging nurturer, and he was the alpha male—quite traditional in a marriage—and although they weren't a couple to hold hands in public, the love between them was immeasurable.

The demise of my warrior mother came fourteen years later. I could say she gave up, but I think really she surrendered, which is a very courageous thing to do. This is where I sometimes say she was selfish because she put herself first and not us. I was relieved that she did. What right do I have to try and make her stay without the love, security and companionship that she craved from my father?

The last few years were the worst. My brother moved into her little bungalow, but this was not a good step. My sister and I, and I'm sure my father from the grave, protested vehemently. This is not because we don't love my brother, but it would create another co-dependent relationship for my mother and we were trying to make a new, independent life for her. My brother helped as best he could, but her warrior stance diminished because now she had no place to stand her ground. My brother took over her house with all his belongings and the projects that he was involved in. Ultimately, she did complain, but it was too late. He had his feet firmly under the table—and in the lounge and the kitchen and every other available room. She was left with the conservatory, where she loved to sit and look out at the garden, and also her bedroom. In the end, she refused to leave the house as agoraphobia and panic attacks re-appeared. I have memories of her suffering from these when I was a child. As often as we would visit to take her out, she would refuse. Even Christmas Day was an effort, but we did finally manage to get her over to us at five in the evening, and then she would relax, and let loose with her Liverpool tongue of humour, wit, and utter cheekiness. Everyone loved my mother; she was such fun. She would take her dentures out and make funny faces in a restaurant, or she would hitch up her top and show us her droopy boobs just because she felt she could.

As embarrassed as we were, this didn't stop her, and we would all crack up laughing, even the waiters!

Love yourself first and everything else falls into line. You really have to love yourself to get anything done in this world.

—Lucille Ball

My mother was never seriously physically ill throughout her life, which is remarkable, because of the lack of self-care she gave herself. She never exercised, hated walking, and would demand to be driven everywhere, even around the block to post a letter or buy more fags. She hated the additional salad provided when she had ordered a sandwich as she thought it was rabbit food. I don't think I ever saw her put a piece of fruit in her mouth, and vegetables were also a very rare commodity, but she loved sweets and sugary things. She didn't drink but loved to smoke and had never heard of plain water. Obviously the quality of her life was pretty dire, and she suffered aches and pains as she got older. She was well known at the doctors' surgery. I cannot count the number of drugs and medications she was on. I don't think she knew either; she would rattle like a shaker, there were so many pills in her body and then of course, when the backache didn't disappear, it was always 'that stupid doctor's' fault. I loved my mother very much, but she was very anxious and negative and worried about things that had not even been thought of yet. Throughout the years I would offer various remedies in an effort to bring her back to life, such as nutritional advice or gentle exercise, acupuncture and alternative therapies. I would attempt to provide healing and positivity in her life. But as I have learned so many times from many of my clients, you can take a horse to water, but you cannot make them drink.

Have you heard these lyrics from an Ed Sheeran song 'Save Myself'?

Life can get you down so I just numb the way it feels
I drown it with a drink and out-of-date prescription pills
And all the ones that love me they just left me on the shelf
No farewell
So before I save someone else, I've got to save myself

One particular client springs to mind. Each week she informs me that she is feeling depressed and fed up, but she has never once acted on any of the suggestions I have put her way. If you want to get better and enjoy your life, rather than endure it, then work must be done. It is your life and your body, and nobody else can run the gauntlet for you.

Keeping my mother alive became a little bit of an issue. She actually died on 11 November 2016, Armistice Day, which was significant as it reminds us very much of our father, who used to spend the entire morning watching the world march towards the cenotaph in London. We felt that this was a definite sign that he was there to meet her when she crossed over.

I was relieved that my mum decided to take off the overcoat that was her skin. The pain and lines on her face literally disappeared once her higher self made that decision and she transitioned to the next dimension. I was pleased for her but miss her physical presence terribly.

My brother has moved to his own place since my mother's departure, and our relationship has improved considerably. The loss he must feel is huge; she was his rock. He and Mum bounced off each other for his entire lifetime. I wonder if that brought more pain than joy, but now my brother tells me very funny anecdotes of their co-existence that I was not aware of, so who am I to judge? Who are any of us to judge or throw stones?

But it does not have to be this way. My mother's nest stopped being empty, but because she lived a life of co-dependency with her father, husband, and then son, she never found herself. Your nest does not have to be full, or shared even, to find harmony. As with the healing school I attended, I learned things from my mother that were not on the syllabus. She taught me many things of which she was unaware.

Of course I understand how easy it is for me to spout out the words on this page as though just reading this book will heal you. It won't. You have to partake, get involved 'get up offa your thang, get up now and do better', as James Brown sings. That song often floats round my mind when I think of certain people who whinge their way through life—you know some of them. But they don't have this book in their hands, whereas you do, so if you have read this far you are on your way, lady!

Nutrition

Let's start with what Mr Bumble, my biology teacher, taught me (and the only thing I remember from his class). *We are what we eat!* But I would hasten to add that we are also what we drink, and water is incredibly important to our well-being. How much do you drink?

There is so much information out there now about what is good for you, and some of it is definitely conflicting. I remember having issues with my body shape in my twenties and followed Rosemary Conley's bible of the no or low fat sermons. Now they are saying we need fat, and I absolutely get that. Of course we do, as we need carbs, proteins, and certain sugars. There are tons of books out there and websites to follow, so I am not going to talk about this too much. Instead, I suggest you take a look at what you eat and write a list. Is there a time of day you need a quick sugar fix? Do you realise that sugar is one of the deadliest poisons on the planet, and it is hidden in so many of our foods? Avoid processed foods so you know what you are putting into your body. Do not microwave your food because you are filling yourself with not just food but also negative energy! Do you eat lots of meat, and where do you get this from? As I mentioned earlier, when we ingest the flesh of another living being, we are also eating their emotions and feelings. If they have not been treated with loving kindness, this will not be a good thing. Believe me. You take in more than just the meat. If you must eat meat, make sure it comes from a local farm or butcher where it has not had to endure cruelty and conditions that no living creature should be put through. If this meat is more expensive than you want to pay, then ration yourself and eat meat three times a week instead of daily. Buy good quality and cruelty free rather than enslaved and maltreated sentient beings.

What about your eggs? Are they happy eggs or are they factory farmed? Are your vegetables home grown or organic? Avoid GMO food at all cost, no matter what anybody tells you. We are not supposed to be messing around with the food that Mother Earth has provided for us. There is enough food to go around, even for the starving people in the poorest countries. It is not the lack of food that is the problem; it is the way the world is run by those in power, so don't feel you need to eat

GMO food to help the planet. That's bullshit. Just as there is enough air for us to breathe, there is an abundance of food. But do we use our lungs fully? Talking of lungs, did you know that they also produce blood and are not just a breathing apparatus? Quite an amazing recent discovery.

... and breathe.

I mentioned earlier an exercise to help use the full capacity of your lungs, known as diaphragmatic breathing, and is very useful as a method to help you de-stress. We tend to breathe in a shallow manner, using the upper part of our chest.

So try this. Find yourself a comfortable position, sitting on the floor or a chair, or lying down with your legs bent so knees are towards the sky. Now place your hands on your lower belly, middle fingers gently touching, and start to inhale through the nose, following the breath to where your hands are. Take your time and slow the breath; then repeat for maybe twenty cycles. Next glide your hands so palms are placed underneath your armpits or across the upper chest and notice your body rise and fall and your sides expand. Breathe slowly for twenty cycles. Finally, glide the hands just underneath the collarbones and breathe in to this area. Feel the back of your ribs push in to the floor if you're lying down. This is a very beneficial way to breathe and slow the system down. We put the body in rest and relaxation mode rather than fight or flight. By breathing fully and correctly, we start to de-stress the system. Spend five minutes practising this exercise before you get out of bed, each day. Although we are what we eat, if we don't breathe, we don't eat! And remember that water!

What other things do you put in, on, or around your body? Do you take vaccinations regularly, such as the flu jab? Is this because someone has told you to; the doctor, the neighbour, the pharmacist, the baker? Why? Look into whether your body really needs to have diseases (vaccinations) pumped into its bloodstream. Fifteen or so years back, my doctor called me up and I thought it was to discuss one of my children. It was. She asked why I refused to give them the MMR vaccination, and I told her my understanding of the damage this jab could do. We had quite an in-depth conversation to include the herd syndrome, but ultimately, because I refused to budge, she removed me from her books because she was not able to reach her financial target. Because I refused the MMR, that was one less drug from Big Pharma that was being purchased at her surgery. It was very difficult for me to find an alternative GP as the majority follow this same procedure, and I believe in Australia there are discussions now about forcing adult vaccinations! They are also jabbing girls at school to allegedly prevent cervical cancer. It the parent refuses, they simply ask the child instead who most likely has no idea about any of this and will go with the majority.

> *At present, intelligent people do not have their children vaccinated, nor does the law now compel them to. The result is not, as the Jennerians prophesised, the extermination of the human race by smallpox; on the contrary, more people are now killed by vaccination than by smallpox.*

> —George Bernard Shaw

and

> *There is a great deal of evidence to prove that immunisation of children does more harm than good*

> -Dr. J. Anthony Morris (formerly Chief Vaccine Control Officer at the US Federal Drug Admin.)

He was discredited which makes me feel his words are even more convincing.

What about the medication that you are taking and I *am not saying to stop* taking these. That would be foolish and irresponsible. I am just saying take a look and find out whether all of it is absolutely necessary. By taking responsibility for your 'self', with love and good health, your lifestyle will start to see a significant difference. And did I mention water? How much fresh, clean water do you consume on a daily basis? If you missed it before, then I've said it again!

We looked at the colour of the clothes we wear in a previous chapter, but have we looked at the fibres that make up these clothes? Are they natural, synthetic, animal?

This is just one chapter touching on self-care, but really it takes a lifetime. The reason we are on the planet is to learn to look after ourselves, and this starts with our own body.

I used to smoke a lot when I was younger, for a period of about five years, maybe forty a day at weekends. Like most youngsters I thought it was cool and a lot of fun, and it replaced my desire to eat. Like many, I had issues with my body size and shape and was constantly yo-yoing. Now I am content with my body shape even though my ego says losing 10 lbs would be a good thing. Maybe it would. But that's not *my* problem; the ego can learn to live with it. I'm quite happy being an endomorph! The first time I gave up smoking, I had visited an acu puncturist and stopped for three weeks. I was joining my mother and sister immediately afterwards, and they could not wait to offer me a cigarette! I declined but after three weeks, I realised I had given up smoking so it wouldn't hurt if I had one, just one.

The second time I went (because I thought the first time had worked), I lay on the couch as he stuck needles in my ears and said, 'once a smoker, always a smoker'. So after that session I immediately went and bought a packet of cigarettes. He was an idiot, but I was the one that made the decision to ignore the work he was doing for me. The third time, I had no choice in the matter because I was going travelling and I couldn't afford to smoke. I had made the decision that this was something I really wanted to do, and I did. After chucking that boyfriend out of my parents' house, this was the second best thing I had done up to that point.

> *Self-care is never a selfish act—it is simply good stewardship of the only gift I have, the gift I was put on earth to offer to others.*
>
> —Parker Palmer

When I got to my fiftieth year, I gave up wine and alcohol, even though that was something I was very good at. I could drink regularly every night and really looked forward to it. The habit came after the babies started to arrive, and it was a release from a hectic day (and night) of mothering. It turned into a habit, which I didn't always understand because there were days I poured a second or third glass of wine which I didn't even want! I would drink lots of Beaujolais, like 'up market' Ribena, but of course I was fooling myself. So I stopped. This was the third best thing I had done for myself because it represented so much to me and I made the decision to knock it on the head. Sometimes we need a reminder that doing the same thing over and over again but expecting different results is insanity. We are responsible for making changes in our life.

> *The woman who follows the crowd will usually go no further than the crowd. The woman who walks alone is likely to find herself in places no one has been before.*

—Albert Einstein

What else are you putting into or onto your body? Shampoos and conditioners, and hair colour—are these natural or are they full of chemicals? Does your toothpaste contain fluoride? Research what fluoride is. You will be horrified.

How do you look after your body? Do you take yourself off for a regular massage? Touch is an incredible healer. Have you considered different styles of massage? Are there other therapists you would like to visit, such as the osteopath, reflexologist, spiritual healer, reiki master, beauty therapist, Rolfer? Take time out to nurture your physical body; it is the only one you have. Maybe book a session to learn about *ayurveda*.

Ayurveda

A true yogi may follow an *ayurvedic* lifestyle, the sister of yoga, which states that we can be categorised into three *doshas* known as *Vata*, *Pitta*, and *Kapha*. *Ayurveda* is an ancient and natural health-care tradition originating in India over 5,000 years ago. It gives us the knowledge of how to live in harmony with our bodies for a healthy, happy, stress-free life, and the word actually means 'the science of life'.

It is based on knowledge of the five elements and three *doshas*, which help to determine our unique constitution. Throughout our lives these five elements (ether, air, fire, water, earth) combine with each other to give rise to the three bio-physical forces (*doshas*) within the human body—*Vata* (air and ether), *Pitta* (fire and water) and *Kapha* (water and earth).

Vata governs movement with the qualities of being light, dry, quick, cold, airy. *Vata* types tend to be thin and are quite tall or quite little. In balance, a *Vata* type is creative and adaptable, but when out of balance, fear and anxiety may arise.

Pitta represents fire and water. Digestion, metabolism, and temperature are controlled by *Pitta*. The qualities of this *dosha* are hot, sour, acidic, and pungent. People who are *Pitta* dominant have good digestion and are athletic. In balance, *Pitta* types are intelligent, logical, and sharp-witted, whereas when they are out of balance they are irrational and easily angered.

Kapha represents earth and water and governs bones, muscles, and teeth. Its qualities are slow, steady, heavy, and cold. *Kapha* types are physically strong with a sturdy build. In balance they are loving, nurturing, and grounded whilst out of balance they can be needy, melancholy, and sluggish in mind and body.

All together, they are known as *tridosha* and govern all the biological, physiological and psychological functions of the mind and body, as well as affecting how an individual interacts with everything around him or her. Every individual has all three biophysical forces, but it is the dominance of any one or two, or even all three, that makes up a person's individual constitution or *Prakriti*.

Although a person's *dosha* type is determined at the moment of conception, *doshas* are constantly shifting within the body. Just as the five basic elements fluctuate within nature, these elements will also fluctuate within the body. Therefore, the *dosha* dominance changes with age, time of day or night, and the season. When the *doshas* become out of balance, physical, mental, or emotional problems arise. *Ayurveda* seeks to treat the mind, body, and spirit according to a person's *dosha* using a variety of treatments, which could include diet, herbal remedies, detoxification, yoga, Ayurvedic massage, and lifestyle changes.

Treatment in Ayurveda is completely unique to the individual as no diet or lifestyle works for all types of people. Once a patient is well, prevention of illness is of vital importance, making Ayurveda a very healthy and beneficial lifestyle choice.

Mantra

Another way to grow, once you have decided to step up and make a change, is to find yourself a mantra. Ask yourself what springs to mind from anything we have discussed that you would like to change about yourself and put it into a short sentence, for example, *I am not sick; I do not smoke; I live life to the full.* It can be anything at all, but once you have found a short sentence that truly resonates with you, stick with it. This will be your mantra. Repeat this over and over in your mind, at every opportunity; when you are brushing your teeth, standing in line, emptying the rubbish. Fill your mind with your mantra until the mantra becomes you.

Believe you can and you're halfway there.

—T. Roosevelt

Things to-do list:

1. Journal what you eat every day for seven days—notice any habits.
2. List your vices. Are there any you are ready to give up?
3. What chemicals do you use on your body (in your shampoo, washing powder, soap, nail polish).
4. Find yourself a mantra and start to use it constantly.
5. Re-evaluate your medications if you take any, and chat with your doctor about them.
6. Book yourself a regular massage or other body treatment.

In the next chapter we help you to realise you are not alone in the feelings you are experiencing, and we practice ways to start re-building another nest.

Chapter 8

WHAT AM I, CHOPPED LIVER? - TAKING RESPONSIBILITY FOR THE EXPERIENCE AND ENERGY YOU ARE HAVING

It's not about how hard you can hit; it's about how hard you can get hit and keep moving forward.

—Rocky Balboa, *Rocky*

W E LIVE IN A WORLD that is full of challenges—and not just the ones that we inflict upon ourselves through relationship or life's general path. The pace at which we live is phenomenal with no punctuation. We send a message out, and before the reply comes we have sent another to someone else. We no longer wait a week for the next episode of our favourite drama; instead, we gorge ourselves on the whole box set like an entire packet of chocolate Hobnobs. OK, maybe not the whole lot but pretty much.

There are so many of us now living on this planet that, particularly in the Western world, we have become impatient, having to wait much of the time. This may be on a phone call to fix our broadband for example, when we are put on hold to listen to music that we don't want to listen to. We are transferred from pillar to post, talking to very polite people a million miles away who are very intent on solving the problem, ma'am. (By the way, did you know you can request to talk to someone in your home country and they will immediately transfer you?) We are told to stand in line, wait here, go over there, do this, and be good. And most of us conform. Then of course, there is the traffic (and parking!)

> *Once conform, once do what other people do because they do it, and a lethargy steals over all the finer nerves and faculties of the soul. She becomes all outer show and inward emptiness; dull, callous, and indifferent.*

> —Virginia Woolf

Our lives can, potentially, be taken out of our own control if we allow this to happen.

In yoga my classes incorporate what I call a Sunday afternoon moment. We do a few stretches then we relax on our mat for a few moments to allow the body and mind to consolidate what it has just done rather than rushing off to the next move, the next item on our agenda. There are not enough Sunday afternoons left in our society, which is not a good thing. Our minds are fully engaged most of the time even if we don't know it, and this piles on more stress and anxiety. A new client has just joined me as advised by her osteopath. Unfortunately, she has developed arthritis, bordering on osteoporosis, and through discussion, she recognises that this has a lot to do with the anxiety she has carried since the age of two! At least she is now on her healing journey, simply by stepping up, recognising, and owning the problem that life has put on her pathway.

When we set the intention to make a change in our life, this is more than a decision and a gentle push using our will power. We are breaking old habits and making new ones. We can create our own destiny, if we want to. We don't have to encounter a preconceived destiny. Are you familiar with Buddha telling us *you must control the mind or the mind will control you?* But sometimes we are afraid of opening our mind; we are afraid of the unknown and even of the fear itself. Most fears are invented. Obviously there are the safety elements of fear like don't stand too close to the edge or you may fall off the mountain, but many of us are afraid of life, and we don't even know it. Fear can hold us back from becoming who we are. When it takes hold of you, ask yourself what it is you are truly afraid of. Frequently ask yourself, *what do you feel and what are you afraid of?*

> *If you are pained by external things, it is not they that disturb you, but your own judgement of them. And it is in your power to wipe out that judgement now.*

—Marcus Aurelius, *Meditations*

Fear or courage

One of my ladies suffers very much from empty nest syndrome, and her children now have children of their own. She is a grandparent but is very lonely. She always arrives late to my class and is the last one to leave, going to the bathroom for at least ten minutes when everyone else has gone home. She will never put her equipment away and sometimes forgets to pay for the class. She is crying out for attention and love as there is a huge void in her life. She often asks to meet for lunch or coffee because, although she moved to be near her grown-up children, they are leading very busy lives and she doesn't know how to fill that gap. It is from this place of emptiness that we can learn and grow because, when everything is running smoothly and we are so busy, we haven't the space to learn.

> *It's often difficult for those who are lucky enough to have never experienced what true depression is, to imagine a life of complete hopelessness, emptiness and fear.*

—Susan Polis Schutz

Whilst writing this book the universe is giving me plenty of examples for illustration. Just this morning I received a call from one of my students. Twenty of us were to go on retreat to a luxurious villa in Tuscany, Italy, to practice yoga, meditation, massage workshops, tennis, swimming, book club, and the list goes on. The trip was a gift. She is a lonely empty nester and loves yoga, so I invited her on the retreat so she could meet like-minded people. Sadly, she called me last minute as she had changed her mind because she didn't want to share a room. You can take a horse to water, remember? Unfortunately, because she is not helping herself and continues to hide inside her old nest, she will become even sadder and more lonely. Sometimes we look a gift horse in the mouth, but we have to make our own choices and overcome that fear. Sod the excuses! There will always be an excuse, whether it's that you don't like swimming, haven't practiced yoga, or dislike sharing a room. Besides, sharing a room might open up new opportunities to make a friend! And there are plenty of earplugs on the market these days.

There is no illusion greater than fear.

—Lao Tzu

Shine your light

Can you identify what you are feeling when a situation outside your comfort zone jumps up and bites you on the bum? What emotions do you recognise? Are they fear, trepidation, excitement, imagination, terror? These are what allow you to feel alive. Remind yourself of this: *The question is not if there is life after death but if there is life before death.*

Of course, sometimes we need help. So now let's jump back to Mr Bumble's class although I didn't learn this from him. As a human being we are an organism, the same as a dog, cat, or sea cucumber, and we humans (not sure about the sea cucumbers) are made up of organs, such as the heart, liver, and lungs. The organs are made up of tissues, which are made up of cells, which are made up of molecules. Stay with me. Inside the molecules we have atoms. And what is inside the atom? Subatomic particles. But if you kept dividing these and dividing again, you would eventually get nothing! Nothing! Just emptiness. Can we *see* the electrons, protons, and neutrons? Possibly under certain conditions, but can we *touch* these things? *No!* They are not tangible.

They float around and vibrate, but they cannot be held, felt, touched, or bounced up and down on our lap. They are energy. Then multiply them by trillions and *they make us*. We are made up of something that you cannot touch. *We are made up of energy, pure light, and vibration.* Isn't that incredible! Research it! When I first discovered that, I was so excited.

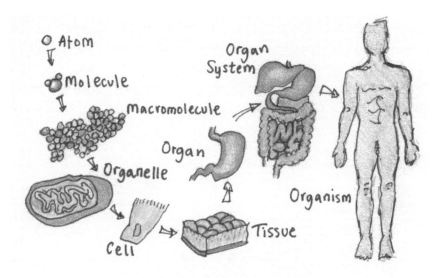

If atoms are made up mostly of 'empty space,' what is in that empty space? Specifically, is there air in the empty space of an atom?

> The space inside the atom is just that, empty space, i.e. vacuum. Air molecules are also made up of atoms with a central core of nucleons and electrons spinning around them. They too have empty space between their nucleons and electrons. One can picture them to be like the solar system with the sun at the centre and the planets revolving around it, with just empty space (vacuum) between the sun and the planets.
>
> —Arun Saha, Staff Scientist, Jefferson Lab (online)

As human beings, we are vibrating at a very low density but we are basically *light beings,* although not all of us act in this way (Hitler comes to mind again).

When we walk into a dark room, we simply flick a switch, and light fills the room immediately. We take this for granted, but it is important to be grateful for this incredible gift of light. (Thank you, Humphry Davy, who invented an incandescent light bulb in 1801 and created the 'arc lamp' in 1809.) At times, *we* are that dark room, and when our switch is turned on we light up, sharing and giving our energy to all and sundry. Like a light bulb, though, there are times we burn out. Perhaps we have not taken care of ourselves, or we are just exhausted, never being allowed to recharge. Sometimes the bulb is not replaced and the darkness continues. This is when our fear kicks in. Although we cannot see, we can feel, and therefore know, that deep down something has to be done. We need a new bulb, but bulbs do not replace themselves. Someone has to assist in the process, and they need help, just like us. Allow someone to help replace your bulb.

One of the fears I had is of falling, whether it be off a ski slope, a horse, or a mountain. I don't think I'm alone in this, but this fear can also protect me as I recognise there are dangers when you fall off a horse. I lived to tell you about it (and it still hurts!) But my fear never stopped me, even though I was clinging on for dear life. The exhilaration I felt when galloping through a meadow on the back of a horse is magical and very spiritual. Another fear I used to have was learning to play tennis; I was so nervous because I thought I was absolute rubbish. I even had to visit the osteopath for treatment for both tennis and golfer's elbow from holding the racket too tightly. I've never even played golf, and I never realised that tennis was such a mind game. I had been too concerned about what people thought and that I couldn't serve properly (still can't). I turned that anxiety into a physical injury—two, in fact! Now I just swear my way through a match and talk a great deal of nonsense, but when I look back, I think I must have been bonkers! How can anyone be frightened of tennis? Easily. Some people are frightened of opening their front door or answering the telephone. Some people are frightened of life.

Flow like water

Fear of the unknown? My family and I were travelling through Madagascar a couple of years ago. It was a bit of a backpacking adventure because I had made all the plans myself without a tour guide, so we knew we were in for a little bit of excitement. Not everything went according to plan, which for me is part of the fun. We had several problems because it is not yet a touristy country, so we weren't able to rely on cashpoint machines, reliable transport, and five-star accommodation. We *could* rely on the people, though, which at first, we were not aware of.

The five of us had been crammed into an overcrowded public bus—full of fruit, boxes, and ducks quacking in baskets—for several hours and were then dropped off to get a small, narrow boat to our next destination. We didn't feel too happy about the boat but had no alternative, so we clambered on board, just our family plus our new-found guide, Abdiasa, his buddy, and the captain! It was a one-way journey taking us to a remote island for a few days to hang out with the lemurs. Remember the movie? We chugged along intermittently as the engine kept stalling but always came back to life. Hey, this is East Africa. 'What about lunch?' my husband enquired. I assured him that little boats would float up to feed us along the way, like the fruit market in Bangkok. Wrong! When I asked our guide, several hours into the journey, if there would be a stop for food, his teeth shone brightly, and within the hour we had pulled up to a local shed with the word *hotel* faintly legible from underneath the grime. This was where the river people live, he explained; they are the poorest of all, and we do what we can to help them. Madagascar is one of the poorest countries in the world, and the average Malagasy makes around $1 US per day whilst 70 per cent of Malagasy suffer from malnutrition. It was an incredible sight. Children splashed around naked whilst fishermen untangled their nets, oxen bathed, and women washed their pans. Within an instant locals descended, carrying beer, coke, (mmm, sometimes, when in Rome) bananas, and smelly fruit. We continued our journey more slowly as the engine trickled along until it became very quiet. The only other sounds of the river were fishermen or villagers getting on with their daily chores. It was too quiet. I turned to look behind at our captain, who was using an oar as were two other people who had silently jumped on board from the river. We used our flip flops and hands. We managed to paddle our way to the river bank, where, once again, white teeth and eyes appeared from nowhere as villagers arrived from within the jungle. We were stranded for many hours as the dark night descended, bringing fireflies and mosquitoes. As poor as these beautiful people were, they were as kind as the kindest I have ever met. For those hours, we happily sang songs with the children and clapped hands. I gave away as much as I could from our luggage to these people in filthy rags with bare feet. My husband taught them card tricks and juggled. I was concerned about the darkness because we were feeding the mosquitoes well that night, but the villagers provided food for us; fresh avocados, fruit, and bananas. I checked with our guide whether we would be able to continue our journey or what the alternative would be, and he simply shone his teeth at me and mumbled something in his broken English. Eventually—out of nowhere, once again—(I felt like writing *Out of Africa*), two men appeared with an engine! This was quite remarkable. They attached it to our boat, and away we chugged into the night, arriving at our next port of call near midnight. We offered to pay for the fruit they provided, but they refused to accept one *ariary*.

From what was one of the most memorable family experiences we have, this could have been the most fearful. Our predicament was quite scary, and nobody had a clue where we were, including us, but the kindness and generosity of the people has instilled in me a sense of utter love and trust for humankind. We were certainly not in control.

When the river is calm, the reflection is clearer. When the mind is calm, there is greater clarity in the field of expression. Our ability to observe, perceive, and express improve. As a result we are able to communicate effectively, clearly, and creatively.

Most of our problems or misunderstandings arise because of a lack of proper communication. When our mind is free from agitation, the way we interact and communicate is so much more pleasant and effective. Our efforts are not hindered by rifts from communication gaps. This leads to a lot of positivity in our outlook and progress in life.

The methods in this book are to help you to turn your light back on, just as Abdiasa continued to guide us to safety—a young man I had never met before, who has now become my friend thanks to continued communication through social media. However, I recognise that with all the distractions in the world and being in relationship, it can be quite difficult to glow, let alone flow.

Learning to give unconditionally through the flow of life—with no agenda, hidden or otherwise—is how you will receive. Experiencing a situation and enjoying it without fear will help us to relax into life and enjoy it for what it is. After all, we are all going to end up at the same front door eventually, so what's the point in creating such a bumpy road when you can float along an African river and see what turns up? So much more fun. This is one reason why I love to teach yoga, to help with flexibility and movement.

Vibrational healing

One way to help you experience this (other than booking a flight somewhere) is to understand a little more about the flow of water. Back to Mr Bumble, I'm afraid. Maybe he wasn't so bad after all (but I didn't learn this from him either). The Japanese scientist Maseru Emoto studied the effects that sound has on water. His early work explored the belief that water could react to positive thoughts and words and that polluted water could be cleaned through prayer and positive visualisation. Something once more to research and I sincerely hope you do.

The average adult human body is 50–65 per cent water. The percentage of water in infants is much higher, typically around 75–78 percent water, dropping to 65 per cent by one year of age. Body composition varies according to gender and fitness level because fatty tissue contains less water than lean tissue.

So if we are made up of water, and it has now been proven that sound can benefit water, what the hell are we waiting for? Remember we found ourselves a really good mantra in the last chapter? Well here's some more information about their benefits.

Mantras that are chanted are basically sound vibrations that permeate every cell of your being and allow your mind to dissolve and repose. Remember, we are vibrating beings (the atom). Certain mantras are sacred to the ancient peoples who believe they have huge benefit to mankind. A mantra is repetitive and so can relieve your mind from worry and anxiety. Often we wonder why we chant some sounds without understanding their meanings. Can something beyond our understanding help us? The meaning of every mantra is infinity. It is a sound vibration beyond the cognition of the mind. When the mind is unable to understand, it simply dissolves and moves into a meditative space. Mantras are as subtle as the air which creates ripples in the water as it gently moves over it. Air is all-pervading and at the same time affects specific regions. Mantras are also all-pervading and create an impact on the one who is practising.

How mantras affect the mind

The mantra is like a seed. Every seed has the potential to become a tree. Similarly, these sound vibrations contain all the possibilities of creation. Some mantras are in the seed form, called *bija* mantras. Others are fully expressed, i.e, the fruit of the mantra is also expressed, such as the Gayatri mantra.

Your mantra is to be kept secret. That which is kept a secret alerts the subconscious mind. Mantras work below the level of consciousness. When we want a seed to sprout, it needs to be sown into the soil, hidden. If it is simply thrown around, birds may eat it. We can read and learn about mantras and their uses, but that will only satisfy the intellect and not translate into experience.

Ultrasound is used in hospitals for various reasons, one of the latest being to help eradicate cancer cells. High intensity, focused ultrasound therapy has proven to be a highly effective cancer treatment in various studies and clinical trials.

So what about music, which can be so healing to our minds, emotions and of course, physical body? If the music is good, happy, and healthy, then the vibration of this sound will permeate your skin and help heal you as well. Heavy and dark music will, of course, do the opposite. I practice meditation using the Tibetan crystal singing bowls, and the experience is quite profound, as the vibrations reach different aspects of our being.

We are three quarters of our way through this book now, and if you have been working through each chapter, I hope you are beginning to feel a difference in your empty nest. Life is like a bicycle, to keep our balance, we must keep moving, so let's continue until you start believing in yourself once again.

Things to-do list:

1. Locate a 'sound/gong bath' in your area to experience the relaxing sounds of the singing bowls.
2. Consider what opportunities you have refused to take up and why.
3. Create a musical playlist that you can listen to regularly.
4. Start chanting your mantra in your mind, with more intention.
5. Name your greatest fear.

In the next chapter we take a deeper look at meditation to see how this can help us find our life's purpose.

Chapter 9

MOURNING HER PAST AND LIVING YOUR FUTURE

I will not cause pain without allowing something new to be born.

—Isaiah 66: 9, The Holy Bible, (New Century Version)

WELL WE HAVE WORKED THROUGH quite a lot in this manuscript in an effort to be empowered so that you realise you have reached a new chapter in your book of life. This is the most important chapter for you to focus on. We have all been put on this earth for a reason, and part of that is to evolve as a human being and a soul—a soul wearing a human body rather than a body possessing a soul. We are spirit until we enter into a human being, when it then becomes a soul. The soul makes us whole (and fills our hole!)

One of the most important roles of a woman, is, without a doubt, to procreate because if we didn't, then obviously that would be the end of the human race. And you have done this! Pretty amazing really and something we just take for granted. Mission accomplished but now it is your time, your turn. By setting your intention, you can manifest the future that you want by living your love and loving your life, and *in being in service to those that need your help.* You are a mother, and there has been a void in your life since your beautiful children flew the nest. But now, from the work we have done together, you can decide where you would like to start, if you haven't already. Do not, under any circumstances, believe that no one needs you, because believe me, *they are crying out for you.* What is the task that you have been put on this planet to accomplish? Now is your time to do just that.

> *You are never too old to set a new goal or dream a new dream.*
>
> —C S Lewis

The title of this chapter has two meanings. One, as you gather your thoughts about your child who has moved away from your home, remember that, once you have given yourself permission to move on to the most exciting part of your life, you will be mourning your past but loving your future. Then, it is time to create this. It is time to be the woman you are supposed to be, and the universe is there to support you. You just need to show up. Well, if you're not excited, I certainly am!

Dreaming up your new directions

We live in a male-dominated society, as I am sure you are aware, but things are beginning to change, as are you, soul sister. There is a masculine and feminine, a black and white to most living things (not an amoeba); there is a good and a bad, a left and a right, a yin and yang. As I have mentioned several times previously, life is about balance. So if it is a male-dominated society, we need to address this. The left side of our body is regarded as the feminine side, so the right is the masculine. When we breathe throughout the day, with gratitude of course, did you know that we alternate the nostrils? For a few breaths we use the left nostril, and then we switch to the right.

We teach alternate nostril breathing in yoga, *nadi shodhana,* which is excellent to calm and centre the mind, release stress, and harmonise the left and right hemispheres of the brain, which correlate to the logical and emotional sides of our personality. The practice works therapeutically for most circulatory and respiratory problems and also helps bring the mind back to the present moment. The *nadis* are subtle energy channels throughout our body, which ensure a smooth flow of *prana* (life force) through the body. I liken them to energetic veins, and apparently, there are 72,000 of them.

So try this: Place your thumb gently on your right nostril. First exhale then inhale through the left. Then close the left nostril with the ring finger and exhale through the right. Inhale deeply into your lungs through the right nostril; then close with the thumb and exhale through the left. Repeat maybe twenty times. Be sure not to block or cover the front of your nose with your hand when you inhale as you want to inhale cleaner air, *prana* (not the carbon dioxide you have just exhaled) which basically is our life force. Keep the mouth closed. You can practice this at the beginning of each day. When we exhale we are removing toxins from our body the same as when we sweat or go to the bathroom, and we encourage breathing through the nose rather than the mouth so that the air has a chance to be cleansed through the hairs in the nostrils like a filter rather than being harshly inhaled directly through the mouth.

In class, when we finish practising relaxation or *yoga nidra,* I ask my students to lie on their left side first and pause because this is less strain on the heart when we rise. The uterus is on the left too, so this is a definite for my pregnant ladies, whether they are in a yoga class or not. And it is much better to sleep on the left because it helps to facilitate lymphatic drainage, makes it easier for the heart to pump downhill, improves elimination, supports healthy spleen function, encourages proper digestion, helps circulation back to the heart, and helps bile flow more freely. There you go! If you suffer from insomnia try sleeping on your left for a few nights and notice any difference. Try *nadi shodhana* as well.

In the UK, we drive on the left-hand side of the road. This is because highwaymen could draw their pistols more rapidly from the left with their masculine right hand to defend against an attacker. Since most people were right handed, swordsmen preferred to keep to the left in order to have their right arm nearer to an opponent and their scabbard further from him.

When I meditate and sit in a cross-legged position, I am always conscious of placing my left hand, female side, on top of my right even though it is natural for me to do it the other way around because I am right handed. We all have male and female characteristics, and my husband once told me there was not enough room for two silverbacks in our kitchen! I can be quite dominant and strong willed, so I am working on my left sidedness to bring me to balance, even though I have been served well with my masculine attributes because I am not afraid to stand up for myself or those I love.

Women have been dominated throughout the ages through culture, religion, business, and virtually every avenue I can think of, but this is the Age of Aquarius, coupled with the new millennium, so changes are definitely coming. I think we are very fortunate to live in such an exciting period. I believe our spirit has chosen this time because the world is in need of light workers. This is you, my lovely, because you are a mother, a giver, a lover, a nurturer, and a woman. It is also probable that your children are born ten or so years either side of the turn of the century and could be classed as *indigo children*. They are here to help turn our planet around, metaphorically speaking!

Your biological changes

I find it quite funny that several bodily functions that pertain only to the female start with a masculine prefix—menstruation, menses, and of course the menopause, which so often comes at the same time as our chicks leave the coup, so we have a double whammy. Quite often the menopause is blamed for many of our mood swings, and justifiably in certain cases. I keep telling my husband that I am still as regular as clockwork, so all my funny turns and adventures are nothing to do with the menopause—he can't wait. But on a serious note, there is help for this wonderful change of life that women go through. It is not a disease; it is just another experience that the human body gets to go through, and I urge you to avoid HRT if you possibly can. There are alternative natural options out there, and diet has a huge part to play in this.

When we go through the menopause—and for some of us, this can be a ten-year period of time—we are letting go of a whole way of life, a regular pattern that no longer serves us, but we are not letting go of our femininity or power. Did you know that at birth we have a set number of eggs in our womb, which we carry until menopause? So when our children flee the nest, we may also be letting go of something else that is life changing. The menopause. Something that we have been used to for many years, maybe a third or half of our lifetime; this is a big change. Take extra, extra care through this life transition. And remember ...

The afternoon of life is just as full as the morning; only it's meaning and purposes are different.

—Carl Jung.

Dreaming up your new directions

You've heard the words '*Quite frankly, my dear, I don't give a damn*' stated by the gorgeous Clarke Gable, right? And the film—of course, *Gone with the Wind*. Fabulous. Did you know that this book was started from the end? Margaret Mitchell wrote it back to front. She knew how she wanted the ending to play out but had no idea what to start with. How cool is that because it is such an epic adventure, and of course, there are a few twists and turns as Scarlett squeezes in and out of her corsets without her desired ending!

So how about it? How about writing the autumn of your life from the end first? Where would you start? Go grab a cuppa something hot and your journal, and give it some thought.

If you could, where would you like to be on the last day of this incarnation? What would you like to have achieved? What would your purpose be? What epitaph would you like engraved on your headstone?

Three further questions:

- What did you love about your life?
- Do you have any regrets?
- If you were given one more chance, what would you do (differently)?

Think about those questions, hold your breath, breathe in some more, and then exhale deeply as you gaze at your new life just over the horizon. Let's recap and put out some ideas if you still haven't found something that totally resonates.

Creativity—reading, writing, drawing, painting, singing, dancing, song writing, learning guitar, drums, banjo, harp, cello, photography, blogging, baking, specialised cooking, fermenting, dressmaking, knitting, weaving, upholstery, ceramics, sculpture, digital artwork, join/create a band or singing group, interior design, write a book, play, movie, poems, quilting, crochet, memoir, record anecdotes from elders, cultivate fruit or bonsai trees, wood carving, learn a new language, attend college classes, join chess/table tennis club, model for life drawing class, stained glass, mosaics, etc.

Physical—walking, running, gardening, jive, belly dancing, flamenco, trekking, sailing, paddle boarding, yoga, climbing, travelling, exploring, adventuring, foreign volunteering, ballet, snow sports, water sports, diving, dog walking, joining an organisation or charity, setting up a new charity, support group, forum, camping, scuba diving, karate, kite flying, learning the Charleston, marathons, skydiving, lollipop lady, open a café, tour guide, rescue animals, become a local or foreign activist, teach English abroad, collect the littered plastic.

Learning or becoming a teacher —Pilates, yoga, reiki, tai chi, chi gong, organising, swimming, technology, astrology, astronomy, numerology, reflexology, massage, acupuncture, psychotherapy, crystal healing, hypnotherapy, meditation, mindfulness, building support groups, coaching, instructing dance classes, mentoring youngsters, nutrition, find your family tree, create a bucket list, educating young people about kindness to animals, children, our planet, TED talks, helping the homeless.

Volunteering—taking any of the above and sharing your existing or new skills with those less able. There are old people, single parents, refugees, homeless, hospices, orphanages, special needs, nursing homes, dementia homes, hospitals, neighbours, schools, abroad, online, family, friends, strangers, and other people that would benefit from your life skills, experience, and light. Be open to what comes to you, as it may not be what you expected.

I think we are all familiar with Gandhi's quote about being the change in the world that you would like to see. Can you imagine how different the world would be if we all did a little bit because, let's face it, there is work to be done. And if you think initiating change is scary, then the way to overcome fear is to get so wrapped up in your new lifestyle that you forget how to be afraid. Logic will take you from one place to another, but imagination will take you anywhere. When you know what you want to do, celebrate in style and plan a party to set you on your way. Set your intention. And remember that the opposite to control is trust.

Healing yourself and our world

One of the juxtapositions that is blatantly crying out for balance is that of light and dark as there is a lot of darkness around us right now. Remember, it only takes one small candle to light up a whole dark room, so imagine the effect an entire tribe of light workers would have, springing up from all corners of the world. This is why we are here at this moment in time; this is why *you* are here. When your soul sat on the cloud up above, chatting away, it was deciding its purpose before entering your body—to help bring our planet out of the chaos that she is now in. As a mother, you can empathise with the pain Mother Earth is experiencing as she continues to be raped, pillaged, and torn apart. We are her children, and look how we are treating our home, our nest. We must look after her, water her, love her—even pick up litter which has been dumped on her.

> *Whether you think you can or you think you can't, you are right.*
>
> —Henry Ford

The world has become a smaller place; chemicals sprayed on one part of the planet impact the other side before the dust has even settled, and we are consuming them in our food. We learn that hibernating bears are being murdered before they leave their cave. We are aware that bees are being destroyed by huge chemical companies that are also poisoning our food. We are also poisoned by chemical trails sprayed into the sky in the name of geo-engineering whilst, below ground, the effects of fracking leak into our water supply. The food that we eat is supposed to help keep people alive, but it is killing us with the interference of genetic modification. The medication they give us is poisoning our systems, as are the vaccinations. Don't misunderstand me because there is a need for hospitals and medication, but so many of us have given away our power to those that are controlling us.

As you know, my first child was an emergency caesarean although I had planned for a home water birth with dolphin music and homeopathic remedies that I had instructed my husband to administer, depending on my symptoms. A backache was pulsatilla, a high-pitch scream was maybe belladonna. In the end he was ramming them all down my throat, and they didn't make a blind bit of difference. Thank God for surgery and the amazing staff at Brighton County Hospital. Otherwise, I would not be here to write these words and bring a further two souls into the world. We have been given a wonderful body that we can roam the planet with, and if we were allowed to use it in the way we were supposed to, we would all be having a happier and healthier life. It is our right to do so. But 'powers that be' know otherwise. This is the truth, and thanks to the World Wide Web, we can search and share and wake up the world, turning on more light. There is so much information out there at the touch of a few buttons, which enables us to wake up to the way the world is being run outside our little boxes. (And there are many more honest search engines other than Google).

This is, in truth, why there is a void in your heart, and you know that something is missing. Perhaps you have a comfortable lifestyle with three meals a day and a warm bed, perhaps a holiday or two a year, but something is missing. You cannot find this missing thing from outside yourself. The missing piece is what lies beneath the skin, within you; this is your purpose. Peace cannot be kept by force, it can only be achieved by understanding.

Make the most of yourself, for that is all there is of you.

—Ralph Waldo Emerson

I briefly mentioned the pineal gland in an earlier chapter. Not many people know much about this, and it is not described in depth in many of the medical journals. There is a reason for this. The pineal gland sits within the depths of our brain, is small and pineapple shaped, and is aligned to our third eye, the *ajna* chakra. Think of where the Hindus place the *bindi* on their forehead.

I mentioned previously how few animals died when the huge tsunami hit Asia a few years ago. Very few animals washed up onshore, apparently. Animals still have their sixth sense; they are not being poisoned or dumbed down by the system (unless they are in factories). Cats actually visit patients in hospices and remain with a patient for a few hours knowing that the soul is about to return to source. Then the person dies.

There is something known as the 'phantom leaf sensation'. When a leaf has been cut, the energy and light of where the leaf was, still remains and can be recorded on film using specialised equipment. The energy of the plant is still there although it cannot be seen by the naked eye. This applies to amputees as well. When a leg has been removed, the patient can still feel pain in that leg, and sometimes energy work/ spiritual healing is required to remove the 'phantom' pain. Remember the aura?

So the pineal gland is our link to source, our sixth sense, and our inner knowing. Unfortunately, like the elements of a kettle, it is being furred up and calcified so that it cannot work as it should. This is occurring through the poisons we ingest, such as fluoride in the water and the chemicals in our diet and in the air. It is being done consciously because we have access to light and power beyond belief, but we are deliberately being dumbed down.

> Our deepest fear is not that we are inadequate. Our deepest fear is that we are powerful beyond measure. It is our light, not our darkness that most frightens us.

We ask ourselves, who am I to be brilliant, gorgeous, talented, fabulous? Actually, who are you not to be. You are a child of God. Your playing small does not serve the world. There is nothing enlightened about shrinking so that other people won't feel insecure around you. We are all meant to shine, as children do. We were born to make manifest the glory of God that is within us. It's not just in some of us; it's in everyone. And as we let our own light shine, we unconsciously give other people permission to do the same. As we are liberated from our own fear, our presence automatically liberates others.

—Marianne Williamson

Think pebbles. By making yourself aware of what is going on in the world, you will start to remove fear from your life and work within your purpose. It is such an exciting time to be alive and contribute to the change that this planet is crying out for. Think movie *Avatar*.

Rubbish food, mainstream news, which, on the whole, are lies; crap TV shows where we watch other people's lives instead of living and loving our own are all intended to dumb us down, and for many people it's working. But if you've got this far in the book, you certainly aren't 'fired'. By all means, choose to relax and watch some of this nonsense. I do occasionally, but I do so with awareness. These days some teenagers are not able to do simple mathematics in their head because of how they are being indoctrinated through the school systems and modern technology (think mobile phones). We are all ultimately looking for enlightenment, to be happy in our own skin, but not everyone is aware of it. It is time to wake up.

Life shrinks or expands in proportion to one's courage.

—Elisabeth Kubler Ross

Alcohol and tobacco are both provided by the authorities to dumb us down and poison us whilst we pay huge amounts in taxes. What positive, healthy, life-enhancing benefits do these give us, other than a feeling of light-headedness and perhaps nausea. On the other hand, there are other natural plants in the universe that have been classed as illegal even though they don't poison or kill us and are non-addictive. In fact, they open up our perception and show us what power we are connected to if only we are allowed to experience it. But they have been tainted, and the majority of the Western world thinks they are bad news. Tell that to the indigenous and ancient peoples. I believe this is because they can be home grown so there is no tax to pay. Also the benefits *some* of these natural plants provide are huge. Of course, this upsets Big Pharma. I am not advocating the use of drugs here, by the way, and for people with addictive personalities, this is a no-go area. Thankfully cannabis oil is being brought back into society so that the oil can be used to cure people of cancer and other ailments.

> *People in the psychedelic trip often experience being at one with the world or even with the universe. It's as if they've gone out to another place. They exist beyond their body. That experience can give them a sense of perpetuity, of permanence, of being part of the cycle of life, which of course, we all are.*

—David Nutt, Professor of
Neuropsychopharmacology, Imperial College London

On occasion, I have taken ayahuasca, which I realise is not everybody's 'cup of tea', but that is exactly what it is—a brew. It's a medicine from the Amazon that is classed as illegal in certain countries, including the UK, so I take myself off to foreign parts for the experience, which is truly an out-of-this-world trip. Sometimes we need different tools to serve us, such as ayahuasca. Once I discovered this, it was as though I had been banging in nails with a shoe when all of a sudden I discovered a hammer. Ayahuasca expands our consciousness for self-therapy.

Our pineal gland makes DMT naturally, which is what ayahuasca contains, so it is not a foreign substance to our body like alcohol or tobacco. It is not a poison; it is not addictive. It is not toxic; it is a natural product. Dimethyltryptamine (DMT) is a tryptamine molecule which naturally occurs in many plants and animals. It can be consumed as a powerful psychedelic drug, historically prepared by various cultures for ritualistic and healing purposes. Rick Strassman labelled it the 'spirit molecule'. The organisation I use when I attend these ceremonies is superb, as they provide a full and thorough integration session for everybody afterwards. This is like receiving fifteen years of therapy in one morning. But as I said, it is not everybody's cup of tea (it even tastes disgusting) although these natural psychedelics have been around long since before we ever were.

When drinking this tea, everybody has a different experience, depending on what that person needs at the time, but it is an occasion to connect with the higher self. Although not always pleasant, for the majority of occasions, I have had an incredible experience and am so grateful to have been provided with this opportunity. The authorities have no right to make this natural medicine, like many others, illegal, but then again they have nothing to gain because we can grow medicinal plants in our gardens without paying tax. So they let us buy cancer-creating tobacco instead, and they make money in the process.

> *Twenty years from now you will be more disappointed by the things that you didn't do than by the ones you did do, so throw off the bowlines, sail away from safe harbour, catch the trade winds in your sails, explore, dream discover.*
>
> —H Jackson Brown

As you start to connect more deeply with your servant heart, your reason for being (besides reproduction), you will realise that there is a lot to do. Take your time in planning, and don't be put off, as there will be times you may wish to become *tamasic* and sit on the couch all day. That's OK. We all need a Sunday afternoon, even if it's Wednesday, but set something up—a list, a plan, a buddy system—so that when you have the off days you know you can get back on track. Depending on where your children are in life, they may wish to actively support you in your new venture, your transition, but do remember: This is *your* purpose, and they will have to discover their own in their own sweet time.

Things to-do list:

1. Practice alternate nostril breathing—*nadi shodhana*—on waking.
2. Write down your life plans, starting at the end. What would you like to see written on your epitaph?
3. Decide what your true soul purpose is, and journal your feelings as you start this new chapter. Build a list, a plan, and maybe find a buddy or create a group.
4. Make enquiries about how you will begin this new adventure and who you could be in service to.
5. Invite some friends around to support you either right away or as you start to make new, like-minded friends. Celebrate. Shine your light and glow!

Our final chapter will be the last step in letting go so you can fill your nest with new life.

Chapter 10

CRYING OVER CINDERELLA (OR NEWLY DISCOVERED LEGO BRICKS)

People are like stained-glass windows. They sparkle and shine when the sun is out, but when the darkness sets in their true beauty is revealed only if there is light from within.

—Dr Elisabeth Kübler-Ross

H AVE YOU EVER FOUND YOURSELF looking for something and then forgetting what it was as you immersed yourself in drawers of old photographs, school reports, and birthday cards? Perhaps you move on to home videos with the intention of de-cluttering your shelf of dusty Walt Disney films saved because you all watched them on replay together. You are amazed that there are any tears left, especially seeing *Cinderella* because when she left her nest, her lifestyle improved tenfold!

These tears you weep are a good thing. Let them flow as another layer of the onion peels away, allowing for happy remembrances and a tidal wave of nostalgia. Enjoy this; enjoy the process, enjoy the emotions, enjoy the feelings, enjoy the energy that surges through you.

When we allow ourselves to be in the moment, we are getting lost in an experience, which could be likened to meditation. We sometimes think that to meditate we have to sit still for a long time and empty the mind. If we can do this, all well and good; however, more often than not, the mind will fill with thoughts and things to do. That's OK because the mind is human and is doing what it is supposed to do. Do not berate yourself if this occurs; just recognise that the mind is going AWOL, and bring yourself back to your meditation. True meditation is to be in stillness, balanced and calm no matter what noises or distractions are going on around us.

Practice stillness and quiet

To meditate, sit or lie comfortably and close your eyes. If you are lying down make sure you are not too comfortable to induce sleep easily. Make no effort to control the breath; just breathe naturally. Focus your attention on the breath and on how the body moves with each inhalation and exhalation. Start for five minutes and build up each week, adding an extra minute or so. Perhaps you can get to a daily meditation practice of thirty minutes. Meditation reduces stress, improves concentration, encourages a healthy lifestyle, and increases self-awareness and happiness. It creates calmness and slows down the ageing process, and it teaches us acceptance. It also benefits cardiovascular and immune health and induces relaxation. The true reason we practice original and non commercialised yoga, is so that we can sit more easily in meditation for longer periods.

I run workshops and retreats where we practice *yoga nidra,* which is a beautiful way to spend forty minutes or so. We find a comfortable position to lie in, warm and safe, and I read a script which connects the mind to the body. This takes you to a hypnogogic place, that gap between the state of being awake and being asleep. The conscious and the subconscious minds merge, and if we surrender to this frame of mind, we can release many negative feelings to the universe, no longer needed in our physical being. At the beginning of the session, we take a moment to set an intention, a *sankalpa,* which tends to be a short sentence, like our mantra. I think you may really enjoy *yoga nidra* if you can find a class near you, or even online, and by all means, contact me.

At the end of my weekly yoga classes, I usually provide a ten minute relaxation period, whereby we have the opportunity to connect with the various parts of our body, offering silent thanks for them as we mentally scan them. This connects mind, body, and soul. It's just a nice way to end the session, in gratitude. The pregnant ladies get an extra long session as they connect with the new soul that has chosen them to be the vehicle to come into this life, sharing two lifetimes, quite an honour and the creation of a new nest.

So giving yourself permission to lose yourself in family videos and photograph albums is a good thing because you release the negative emotions your body has been holding onto at a cellular, emotional and maybe energetic level. You thereby create a space to invite something new and good and happy to fill that void. If you find that you are crippled by the pain of this reminiscing, then I suggest you make this a part of your daily or weekly routine until the sadness begins to melt away. It will.

> *Letting go allows us to live in a more peaceful state of mind and helps restore our balance. It allows others to be responsible for themselves and for us to take our hands off situations that do not belong to us.*

> —Melody Beattie

Whilst sorting through your 'stuff' and beginning to de-clutter, is there a certain image, photo or card that pulls at your heart strings more powerfully than the rest? Take these and make yourself a little collage of all those beautiful memories, which you can place in a prominent position in your home to walk past regularly. Those tears of sadness will change. Ultimately, as you get used to seeing this collage of family memories, the emptiness in your heart will be filled with joy, love, and gratitude for the wonderful moments which you shared with other human beings.

Take this one step further and write a letter to your children telling them how you feel, how you felt then, and how proud you are that they have gone off into the world to live an independent life. If there are any negative feelings, then it is important to get them out of your system, else they could produce a nucleus of anxiety. So release everything sooner rather than later to prevent any further guilt or anxiety from developing. This will help you clear the way so you can move on. You don't have to post this letter unless, of course, you want to. Keep it, treasure it, or make a ceremony of burning or burying it and offering it with thanks to Mother Earth, *Pachamama* as the Native Americans say.

Practice intentions and gratitude

Gratitude is a very powerful emotion and something we don't always recognise. Quite often, because we lead such busy lives, we take objects, people, and situations for granted without any sense of thanks towards them. It is in giving that we receive.

If you thank Me, I will surely increase you.

—Ibrahim, 1: 7, Quran

And

Give to everyone who asks of you, and whoever takes away what is yours, do not demand it back.

—Luke 6: 30, The Holy Bible (New Century Version)

A friend of mine had a reason to be grateful as she had pulled herself through one of life's rich challenges involving her health. She made a full recovery, and part of her healing was to find a reason to be grateful every single day she was given after her diagnosis. She cut out strips of coloured paper and wrote a reason to be grateful—something simple such as the air that we breath, the food that we eat, the stranger who smiled at her—so that by the end of the year, she had 365 reasons to be cheerfully grateful. She was reminded constantly as she linked them together each day, creating a gratitude chain which she hung throughout the walls of her house (just in time for Christmas!)

Hopefully, your offerings of gratitude will include the children you brought into this world, who may have now turned into strong and independent young adults. Be mindful and grateful for the strength you have in bringing up these young human beings and the wonderful qualities you have instilled in them. When I expressed my pride to my daughter about her elder brother this morning, as he travels the world on a shoestring living a life that he wants to rather than being caught up in a 9–5, she said, 'well, that's the way you brought him up, Mum.' I was so grateful for my three children at this point that secret tears flowed quietly.

By creating gratitude we are sending positive messages out to the universe and working with the law of attraction. We discussed earlier that we are actually vibrational beings and the thoughts that we deliver will resonate with the universe, be these good or bad, so be careful what you wish for (let alone what you say or think!) The law of attraction is one of life's biggest mysteries, and very few people are fully aware of how much of an impact it has on their day-to-day life. Whether we do it knowingly or not, what you have become is what you have thought so that every one of your experiences in life, good or bad, has been shaped by you and you alone! Read that line again!

By working with this law, we can write down the items, situations, even lifestyle that we would like to invite into our lives. When practising this law, we do not want to be too specific. In other words, concentrate on the actual feelings you wish to create from your desire rather than the physical description. You may wish for a tall, dark, handsome stranger to appear in your life, but he could turn out to be an axe murderer. Instead send out the desire for an attractive and compatible companion who will share similar interests with you so you have fun together, or maybe set this intention with your current spouse. Instead of demanding to see your offspring every Sunday, may I suggest you request to spend more quality time with your children. Get the picture? Then, when you have set your intentions, don't dwell on them. Let these new eggs start to fill your nest once again.

I know this works. Like many, I had always wanted to create monetary wealth and I did not want to work for someone else to be told what to do for an hourly rate. I always wanted a passive income to give me freedom to do what I wanted to do with my life. On de-cluttering some boxes a few years ago, I rediscovered a diary in which I had written thirty years previously. I had sowed a seed of my desire to have a property portfolio which would allow me to be financially independent. I showed (sowed) this seed of consciousness openly to the universe and then got on with my life, travelling the world, having fun (at times with no money whatsoever) and building my nest. I now own a large number of rental properties, and my husband and children have also started to build their own portfolios.

You can sow your own seeds of intention and, in the process, make it a fun activity to ensure it works. Create for yourself a vision board or a beautiful box or even a special shrine to invite the people, objects, and lifestyle you desire into your future. Take time to go through magazines, cutting pictures out for your next dream holiday destination or a beautiful harp that you would like to learn to play or a fit and toned body. Anything that you would like to attract into your life, just add to your vision board. And then get on with your life on the understanding that you have all you desire already, no lack, and see what turns up. However it knocks on your door, be grateful!

> *Whatever you do or dream you can do – begin it. Boldness has genius and power and magic in it.*

> —Johann Wolfgang Von Goethe

Finding our new bearings in new places (either physically or in life)

Of course, it was not always like this. There have been many, many times when I had no money at all—literally. At nineteen I had been working on a kibbutz in Israel for several months and then travelled across the country and into Egypt. As students and backpackers know, money is always at the top of your mind because there is such a lack. Knowing that I had no money kept me in that state of being. *Poor!*

I was standing at the foot of the Great Pyramid in Giza with a group of people when a very old Egyptian with only one working eye approached me and asked if I would like to visit the Queens Tomb, which was closed to the public. Now to this day, I have no idea why he chose me, but I am eternally grateful because I accepted his kind, generous, and free offer. I had no money to spare and he never asked for any. After this incredible and privileged invitation, I learned that this kindly gentleman was a local celebrity nicknamed 'Champion' because he held the record for racing to the top of the Great Pyramid (when it was allowed) in the quickest time. He was also the royal and official guide, so how honoured was I when he invited me to stay in his home for as long as I cared to! I was travelling with Sam, a Dutch friend who was sceptical and initially said no, but my friend Julie was happy to trust in my decision and jumped at the opportunity. Ultimately, Sam slunk up behind us, dragging his dusty feet. We hadn't eaten properly for days due to lack of funds, but we ate like royalty whilst staying with Champion. The first meal was couscous, which I had never heard of and disliked enormously, but I was so grateful to be fed. The second night he asked if we liked chicken. In those days I was not vegan so it sounded like we would be celebrating Christmas early, I was so hungry for a roast dinner. We could hear the poor creature being chased round the courtyard before his wife caught it, despatched it, plucked it, cooked it, and served it to us. We spent many happy nights in his yard watching the locals come and collect water, balancing jugs on their heads because his was the only supply in the whole of Giza at that time. Even the Hilton Hotel opposite did not have flushing toilets or running taps. He insisted we wear his Egyptian robes, which proved very comfortable. We had such fun climbing the pyramids each day and night, and he would encourage us to sit in silence as he did when he took us into the desert to meditate. I had no idea what meditation was until then. And then there were the times we would smoke the hubbly bubbly late into the night and sleep under the sky with millions of stars for a blanket.

Sadly, Champion passed away a few years ago, but I did visit him again when I was pregnant with my first son. Giza had transitioned into a world of mayhem due to the mass increase of tourists and commerce. When we stepped off the bus, I asked a local where I could locate Champion. 'Champion, you are friend?' this stranger enquired. The parting of the crowds was like the Red Sea as everyone stood aside to let us walk through and then followed us to where Champion's humble home had became a large shop with fluorescent lights and busy-ness. It was a wonderful moment and he looked exactly the same. I am so very grateful to this wonderful, gentle, and kind man who taught me so much. His true name was Hefnawi Adel Nabi Fayed, and he was eight when he first scampered up the massive blocks to the top of the Great Pyramid. 'The day I stop talking about the pyramids and the Sphinx is the day I want to die,' he once said. I have since visited many pyramids around the world and I do not believe what the history books have told us.

I read somewhere that God gives every bird its food, but he does not throw it into its nest. I am aware that I have been fortunate to experience many similar situations from people around the world, who have shared whatever they had with me when all I could pay in return was a smile or a few words of thanks. One lesson I learned was to trust, not just in people but in the universe. There is always enough, but be open to how it is presented to you. If it is not the way you like it, then there is a reason for that. As I said earlier, we are given lessons in life to grow from, and if we do not learn them the first time round, they will repeat themselves until we get the message. Lessons I learned from Champion are of kindness, generosity, trust, and spirituality, and I try to practice these in my own life. I have also tried to instil these vital qualities within my own children. I didn't know it then, but he was my guru.

Another act of kindness that remains with me was when I was backpacking in Asia, staying in a youth hostel up many hundreds of steps. This was in Hong Kong, where people from all over the world joined for a moment in time before heading off in their own directions. We had all been discussing the fact that we were broke; hence, we always walked the hundreds of steps rather than hire a taxi to take us 269 meters above sea level. A lovely young American woman sat opposite me on our bunk beds and very simply handed me a beer. I was not sure why she did this. Hey, what goes around comes around, she said. That was the first time I had heard the expression, and her gentle act of kindness has stayed with me forever. Whenever I see someone in need, I will share, be it time, a smile, or a donation to a person who appears homeless.

In London I recently handed a destitute young Eastern European a £20 note whilst he shivered on his damp cardboard in front of a large plastic recycling container on Tottenham Court Road. He looked so poorly that, the second time I saw him, I offered him food and asked if he would like help. He refused both. I was quite upset that in this allegedly civilised country, human beings could find themselves in such a dreadful predicament. The third time I saw him was different. He was standing tall and upright with no sign of shivers, talking to a friend who was about to take his place on a fresh piece of cardboard. My shivering destitute friend then skipped across the road and jumped energetically into a waiting car! It was definitely a scam, and part of me was furious, but then I reminded myself that my act of kindness is what was important—my thoughts and my intention, not the outcome. *What goes around comes around.* I truly believe and feel I have experienced this. I think it says we reap what we sow, somewhere in the Bible, which I believe without any doubt whatsoever.

For people who create scams, I feel a degree of sadness. I have no idea what drives people to 'steal' money or anything else from another, but it obviously comes from a feeling of lack, of not having enough in life, whether this be money, food, love, time, or who knows what. At the end of the day, some people are forced to take from others because, at this stage in their soul's journey, they know no other way. I do believe that, through many lifetimes, we learn how to act in a way that is right.

In yoga, the term is known as *asteya,* meaning non-stealing. I don't want to bring myself down into negativity by judging another human being by their actions, and I will not feel angry that someone has conned me out of money as I don't see it like this at all. Money is a tool to help me live the life that I choose to live. I have enough to feed myself and my family and to pay my bills. I have enough to do the things I want to do in my life, and that includes sharing it with others I meet who are needier than me. I don't take it for granted because one day that needy person could be me, as it was in my younger days.

In yoga there are three different types of attitudes in which the mind functions. These are called *gunas,* and we all carry an element of each one. *Tamasic* (as mentioned in a previous chapter) implies inactivity, someone who is not particularly spiritual or 'awake' and focuses their interest on him or herself, but the mind is never at rest. It is always discontented and disturbed. These people tend to be less active, perhaps sitting on a sofa much of the day, stuffing pizza and drinking beer! They wouldn't be interested in charitable duties. Life for this person is like driving a car with the breaks on. The attributes are negative.

Someone who is *rajastic* is more active and caring and can never keep quiet, constantly racing, procuring, and wanting more and more. Strength is a prime quality, and they tend to be energetic doers. For this person life is like driving a car with no brakes. They give charitably but would like to tell the world about it. The attributes are neutral.

Then we have *satvic* people, those who have a steady mind, free from agitations with peace and happiness. This is what we are all aspiring to be as we wind our way up towards enlightenment, where we are aware and spiritually connected. We may give to charitable causes but don't feel the need to share this with anyone. Life for the *satvic* individual is like driving a car with power steering and power brakes.

Can you see any of these qualities in yourself or anyone around you? The aim is to become more *satvic* through each of our incarnations so that one day we have no need to return to earth, as we've learned all life's lessons. Yoga does seem to thread its way through everybody's tapestry without ever having to stand on a sticky mat. But there are many roads to find peace and inner happiness.

When we travel along this wondrous path called life, we have no idea what is in front of us; we can only look back. When we climb mountains, we don't know how we are going to get to the top. We just know that the top is our destination, so, when we start to climb, we place our feet where they fit. As we walk through life, we use proprioception, which means the place in space that our body takes up. We do not consciously look down at our feet to make sure we lift and lower each foot separately and safely; we trust that the ground will be there to hold and support us. Perhaps there are times when we don't pay attention and we fall, but we get back up and always carry on. Trust in *your* process, trust in your feet, trust in the sensations of the body, and trust in the universe. I truly believe that we can attain our full potential with the help of silence, meditation, and non judgement, plus a whole lot of gratitude and intention thrown in. And of course, the most important one of all, forgiveness. How about you?

> *When you dance, your purpose is not to get to a certain place on the floor. It's to enjoy each step along the way.*

> —Dr Wayne Dyer

Things to-do list:

1. Purchase some colour strips of paper and create your gratitude paper chain.

2. Decide on your vision board, box, or shrine, and start bringing into your life the things that you want to create for your new lifestyle.

3. Practice meditation—there are many different types, including walking and mindfulness.

4. Find a *yoga nidra* class or video where you can work more deeply with your *sankalpa*.

5. Write a letter to your children and release it to the universe.

Conclusion

In this book I have attempted to illustrate that you have a purpose beyond parenthood and nest building—one that is crucial to your well-being as well as to your fellow human beings and our planet. You have a purpose and your soul, your higher self, knows this. I am just trying to jog your memory so you can find out what it is that you came to do. Once you connect with it, you will know, so if it doesn't appear to be the first thing you try, please do not give up! Keep going until you get there. It doesn't have to be something huge. Knitting cotton hats for refugees or reading poetry to a blind person is a purpose. You will be changing someone's world and making a difference. My wish for you is that when you find your reason to be in your skin, your life becomes so full to the brim that it overflows.

You now know yourself, what your next thing is to do and I hope you are *uber* excited to get on with it, so I won't chat for too much longer.

I would love you to make contact with me and let me know how you are getting on. I want to learn of your success and I want to help, so if you feel the desire to get in touch with me, please do.

This workbook is a course in itself. However, I realise obstacles and distractions may arise even if you follow the formula. But remember, I am here. Also, some of us may still have children at home, but continue to feel the emptiness. The Empty Nest. Likewise, some of us have an empty nest without ever having giving birth. So please don't think these lessons are just for parents. We all have a true purpose in life, we simply have to go out and find it!

> *To be consistently effective, you must put a certain distance between yourself and what happens to you on the golf course. This is not indifference, it's detachment.*

> —Sam Snead

Likewise, I am sure you would agree that a surgeon should not be weeping into an open wound. Give it some thought!

Thank you so much for taking the time to read these words. From the depths of my heart, I wish you peace, joy, and total fulfilment as you continue your wondrous journey on this beautiful blue planet, Gaia, Pachamama, Mother Earth.

Namaste
Kizzi x

Acknowledgements

I would like to acknowledge my next-door neighbour of many years passed, who inspired me with a few words across the garden wall. Thank you, Jane, as you encouraged me to always take time out for myself when I became a new and very inexperienced mother. Your words have stayed with me.

And of course, my wonderful family; my husband and children, with whom I have built our nest, which will always be a home to our three children (and maybe theirs one day). Then of course, my lovely sister, who is also my bestie.

I would also like to thank my niece, who created the artistic offerings in this book. including the book cover. Thank you, Fifi! x

About the Author

Kizzi has three young adult children and lives at the foot of the South Downs in Sussex with her husband, two dogs, one cat, two Shetlands, and Dylan the llama. She left home at seventeen with some cash in her pocket and a pack on her back to travel the world for seven years. At twenty-five she returned to England, where she settled down to build her nest with her husband.

She is a trained healer, hypnotherapist, and yoga teacher. She volunteers with Childline and local homeless charities. She travels abroad frequently and is currently involved in building schools in Sierra Leone and other third world countries. She has subsequently set up a charity called Friends of Chema and Kizzi. Get in touch if you would like to get involved or volunteer. She loves to explore, play tennis, walk, write, sing, laugh, and dance. She also runs wellness and volunteering retreats around the world.

Kizzi is currently studying for a degree in psychology and philosophy with the Open University.

To contact Kizzi, visit her website at:
www.kizzithefreerangemama.com

Lightning Source UK Ltd.
Milton Keynes UK
UKHW042101021118
331661UK00001B/6/P